KU-020-620

ADVANCE PRAISE

"Groundbreaking, fascinating, and sobering. Finally—we have an explanation. This seminal work of Dr. Valerie Rein is a must-read for every woman in the process of unlocking her own ultimate fulfillment and success."

—ALI BROWN, CEO, ENTREPRENEUR, MENTOR

"The greatest barriers for women now and ahead are internal. Especially as the gender equality movement adds more responsibility to women's plates—we need a new movement that gives women the tools to manage and optimize their mental health so they can rise in leadership with greater ease and joy. Dr. Valerie has some of the most groundbreaking solutions I have seen. Whether you're in the corporate or entrepreneurial world, starting out or advanced in your career, this is a must-read for all women."

—CLAUDIA CHAN, CREATOR OF S.H.E. SUMMIT, AUTHOR OF *THIS IS HOW WE RISE* LEADERSHIP BOOK, PODCAST, AND COURSE

"Mind-blowing. I was immediately impacted by Dr. Valerie's definition of trauma. I have it so great. I am blessed. I have a good family. I'm lucky for a life of opportunity. These messages blind us to years of trauma that impact every single area of our lives. Not to mention the trauma we carry from our ancestors and the collective trauma of women today.

Through beautiful storytelling, facts and research, and heartfelt relation to what is really going on in our lives, Dr. Valerie creates a transformation. From that feeling of something not being quite right, to understanding, to actionable steps, and finally to power, Patriarchy Stress Disorder is required reading for women if we are to realize our power and impact our world. THANK YOU Dr. Valerie for the work you are doing for women and for our world!"

—CARRIE SECHEL, FORMER DELOITTE PARTNER, BUSINESS CONSULTANT, AUTHOR, SPEAKER

"Dr. Valerie is the go-to expert on identifying and healing the complex effects of intergenerational, cultural, and personal traumas that all humans carry. These have a profound impact on how we show up in life and at work and how we work with each other. The fields of human resources and diversity, equity, and inclusion and anyone concerned with advancing equality and empowerment should be paying attention to Dr. Valerie's work."

—JENNIFER BROWN, FOUNDER, PRESIDENT, AND CEO, JENNIFER BROWN CONSULTING (JBC), AUTHOR OF *INCLUSION* AND *HOW TO BE AN INCLUSIVE LEADER*

"As a single mom I resonated with the constant guilt and fear of passing along my issues to my twin girls. After reading this amazing book, I now will focus on being unconditionally OK with myself and passing that on to my girls. Instead of the way I have been surviving my life, I want to thrive—and now I have a way to do it!

This book is a masterpiece. Just like a really good movie, its message sticks: how good can it get? It inspired me to take a new direction with my team and we had a great meeting this morning. We agreed to work together to change from being reactive to proactive! Thank you Dr. Valerie for sharing the light with us!"

—DR. JILL WADE, OWNER OF STONEBRIAR SMILE DESIGN

"We can't untie the knots we cannot see. In this brilliantly written and courageous book, Dr. Valerie Rein makes visible the web of knots that hold us back. Her writing captures your imagination and your heart and takes you for a ride through your own history of setbacks and self-limiting behaviors. Join the women Dr. Valerie has helped break through the chains of PSD by reading this amazing book. The stories, research, and practices in Patriarchy Stress Disorder will inspire you to live from your best self. I could not put this book down, and I learned something new about myself on every page. Thank you, Dr. Valerie!"

—AMY WEINTRAUB, FOUNDER OF LIFEFORCE
YOGA, AUTHOR OF YOGA FOR DEPRESSION
AND YOGA SKILLS FOR THERAPISTS

"Dr. Valerie helps us better understand the invisible programs encoded in our DNA that subconsciously affect us. Corporate executive women, especially in healthcare, are affected by cardiovascular disease, weight gain, eating disorders, addiction, depression, anxiety, issues with sleep, and ultimately burnout. Backed with eye-opening data, Patriarchy Stress Disorder uncovers the invisible root of the issues that plague powerful women and offers scientifically informed exercises that readers can begin putting into practice immediately. I would love to see PSD included in every psychology textbook."

—DR. ANNE ARVIZU, CEO, RXER COMMUNICATIONS CORP.

PATRIARCHY STRESS DISORDER

PATRIARCHY
STRESS DISORDER

THE INVISIBLE INNER BARRIER TO
WOMEN'S HAPPINESS AND FULFILLMENT

VALERIE REIN, PHD

LIONCREST
PUBLISHING

COPYRIGHT © 2019 VALERIE REIN, PHD
All rights reserved.

PATRIARCHY STRESS DISORDER
The Invisible Inner Barrier to Women's Happiness and Fulfillment

ISBN   978-1-5445-0577-0 *Paperback*
       978-1-5445-0578-7 *Ebook*

Back cover headshot by Margie Woods.

\

CONTENTS

INTRODUCTION

When we see the invisible, we can do the impossible.

—ANONYMOUS

I WAS ON THE PHONE WITH A CLIENT WHEN I SUD-denly noticed I was only smiling with one half of my face.

The right side of my mouth lifted up, but the left side wasn't cooperating. By the time I got off the phone, my left arm wasn't working, either. It just hung there. I thought, *that's funky. What's going on?* With my right thumb, I typed "weakness on the left side of the body" into my phone. I read the word *stroke*. I got in my car, and using my right arm, I drove myself to the emergency room.

Within minutes, I was hooked up to what felt like every beeping and monitoring device they could find. Thus began a multi-hour adventure to understand what was wrong with me. As I was examined and tested, I progressively felt better. I was being taken care of. The staff wheeled me around on a stretcher through the doors that opened automatically. They covered me with blankets before entering a cold room. They brought me water before I had to ask. They waited on me hand and foot and smiled reassuringly. I felt like I was at the Ritz-Carlton—the only other place on Earth where I'd ever experienced my needs reliably and consistently met and anticipated.

There were no calls to answer. No one to take care of. There were no demands on me. Except to lay there and breathe. I was guilt-free; possibly for the first time as a mother, wife, and professional. A stroke scare quailed at me for a hall pass. Surrounded by the soft meditative beeping of the machines, I began to relax and enjoy my spa day in a hospital gown.

Thankfully, all the test results came back normal. It was "just stress" that had taken my left side temporarily offline. They let me check out to go home.

I looked at the clock and realized I could still make my evening client appointments. I changed into my civilian clothes, drove to my office, and held my evening sessions as though nothing had ever happened.

Such is the power of the status quo. If I wasn't dead, I was working.

Can you relate?

Countless high-achieving female clients over the years have shared with me about their burnout, their frustration, disillusionment, despair, rage, depression, adrenal fatigue, issues with weight, digestion, and sleep, panic, and anxiety.

"I grapple with a constant feeling of overall exhaustion, because I feel like I always have to just keep dancing."

"I'm afraid of failure. I have to be the best at all times, and always be pleasant and leave everyone smiling."

"I wake up anxious. My heart and my mind are racing at the thought of everything I need to do. I force myself to meditate, but it doesn't really work, and I feel like a failure."

"I just want to wake up in the morning feeling happy."

It was easier to see in them what I was struggling to see in myself. We high-achieving women keep pushing until we break, until we're stopped dead in our tracks by crises in our health, work, or relationships. Only when we're up against a wall do we finally see the prison we're in.

But what is this invisible inner prison? And what crimes got us there?

REDEFINING TRAUMA

Over the years of my work as a therapist and in social conversations, I've been hearing women express the feeling of being stuck, imprisoned. Women talked about wanting more—more intimacy in their relationship, more impact of their work in the world, more fulfillment in life, feeling more comfortable in their skin, more peace and happiness. They expressed frustration, feeling like as they try to reach for this *more*, they are running into an invisible inner wall.

These women did not just spend their lives daydreaming. For years, they worked hard on doing everything our culture told us we've got to do to earn our happiness and fulfillment. Be a good girl. Do well in school. Work hard on your career. Get married. Buy a house. Raise children. Own nice things. Take vacations.

And when checking off these milestones on the map did not take them to the promised land, they looked within. They read self-help books, attended personal growth workshops, seminars, and retreats, tried yoga and meditation, as well as therapy and medication. And still they were not where they wanted to be.

Before my stroke scare, like all of my clients and other high-achieving women I knew, I was rocking the prison life. From the outside looking in, I had it all: a thriving private psychology practice in New York and a global coaching and consulting business. Two graduate degrees in Psychology (yes, I was *that* troubled)—a master's from Columbia University and a PhD from the Institute of Transpersonal Psychology. I had a prestigious job at a major university and taught in a master's in counseling program. I married a good man, had a wonderful daughter, and bought a nice house in a suburb of New York City. The ER episode pierced through the nice facade of "having it all." I was confronted by the fact that I did not *feel* as happy and fulfilled as I looked on paper. I finally began to catch the glimpse of my invisible inner prison. When one half of my body fell silent, I finally began to listen to the parts of myself that I had been too afraid to hear from before.

I began wondering: how come my clients were making these big shifts in their lives? They were transforming their careers, businesses, health, and relationships. From being at the mercy of anxiety, anger, and addictions—to joy, peace, and contentment as their new normal. While I still felt stuck. What was I doing for them that I was not doing for myself?

And then it dawned on me. With all of my clients, I was using mind-body tools for trauma healing. Even with those who did not think they had any unresolved trauma. Inevitably, when we took a closer look under the hood of what was driving anxiety, depression, feeling lonely in her marriage or trouble meeting a partner and creating a fulfilling relationship, difficulty with arousal and orgasms, unwanted weight gain or loss, self-soothing with food or alcohol and other addictive behaviors—we found trauma.

The reason I was not doing it for myself was...*I did not think I had any trauma.*

Ironic, I know. But you can probably relate to my confusion. In fact, you may be thinking that *you* don't have any trauma.

The reason is that the conventional definition of trauma ties it to witnessing or experiencing a life-threatening event. It makes us think of combat, rape, and domestic violence. But why then did all these people who've never experienced or witnessed a life-threatening event have symptoms of trauma and respond so well to mind-body tools for healing it?

Because they're human, like you and me. My experience of being human and helping humans heal has clearly shown me that *all* humans have trauma.

Others before me have recognized that most kinds of trauma, in fact, do not fit into the narrow conventional definition. Trauma-healing practitioners distinguish between the capital T and the lowercase t kinds of trauma. Among the latter are adverse childhood experiences and many other events humans commonly go through that often result in lasting traumatic effects.

My personal and professional journey has led me to broaden the definition of the lowercase t trauma even more. I define trauma this way:

> *Trauma is any experience that made you feel unsafe in your fullest authentic expression and led to developing trauma adaptations to keep you safe.*

This includes any event that caused you to dim your

light, any situation that made you withdraw from being fully yourself. This circumstance might have come in the form of an insult, a glare, an offhand comment that you're too big for your britches, or unwanted sexual attention. If thinking of it now makes you shrink a little inside, it's probably trauma.

Trauma adaptations are protective mechanisms that are created in response to trauma. They're meant to keep us safe, and they do so by keeping us in an invisible inner prison. The prison walls are made of the traumatic experiences, and trauma adaptations act like prison guards. They operate in our minds, bodies, and actions—creating thoughts, physical challenges, and self-sabotaging behaviors that block us from moving forward and experiencing what we truly desire.

"STOP HOLDING YOURSELF BACK!" AND "WHAT'S WRONG WITH ME?"

Much like Rapunzel's Mother Gothel, the prison guards convince us that staying locked up is the only way to stay safe from the dangerous world out there. An important note: most trauma defenses operate on the subconscious level. Consciously, we may feel very confident, competent, and not at all think of the world as dangerous. However, the trauma imprints in our bodies and minds activate the defense systems regardless of what we consciously believe. These are the invisible walls that we run into when we reach for *more*—more happiness, intimacy, or impact—because the vulnerability they require touches the original trauma, making us feel unsafe. When our traumas get triggered, the walls go up and stop us dead in our tracks.

You may have heard the awful slogan popularized by the self-help, "self-improvement," personal development, motivational speaking, and coaching industries that implores you to "Stop holding yourself back!" What makes this phrase so awful is that it suggests that people—mostly women, who make up at least 70 percent of the self-help market[1]—are consciously choosing to hold themselves back. It puts us on the hamster wheel of "self-improvement," where we keep trying our hardest and running our fastest to "stop holding ourselves back."

This is as futile as it is heartbreaking. The most painful casualty of this race is our confidence—because no matter how hard we try and how fast we run, we don't seem to be able to succeed at "not holding ourselves back." We're left with the shame of yet another perpetual failure, pondering the patriarchy-old question every woman habitually asks herself: "What's wrong with me?"

I wrote this book to show you that there's *nothing* wrong with you and that you're *not* holding yourself back.

What's holding us back is the invisible prison of trauma lodged in our subconscious. It's not your doing, it's not your failing, and it's not something that's "wrong"

---

1   "The Market for Self-Improvement Products and Services," *Market Data Enterprises,* 2017.

with you. It's not a "mindset" issue that you need to "fix." Holding us back is how the trauma prison operates. Self-help hacks not only fail as a lasting solution—they typically backfire. The only way out of the invisible inner prison is to uncover and heal the trauma that erected it. Let this sink in. For me, my clients, and every other high-achieving woman I've talked to about wanting more and running into an invisible wall, our suffering is exacerbated by our shame about feeling this way. Maybe you, too, are exhausted from having to fend off the shame attacks along the lines of "What's wrong with me, why can't I just snap out of it?" "I have a good life, why can't I just be happy? What's wrong with me?" Maybe you, too, have been coping with the pain by numbing it with work, food, drinks, shopping, social media, or streaming shows. Maybe for you, too, this coping has been giving rise to more shame and more agonized questioning: "Why can't I just put down the spoon and put the ice cream back in the freezer? What's wrong with me?"

"What's wrong with me?" is the question a woman asks herself again and again. We feel alone in our suffering. Because other women don't talk about theirs. Because they are ashamed, too. Because they "should" be happy—their lives are so good. Which confirms our worst fears, that something *is* wrong with us.

My message to you, that this book will unpack, is that *there's nothing wrong with you*. There are invisible, unrecognized traumas in our lives. Trauma adaptations that developed to protect us, form an invisible inner prison that holds us back from living a full and thriving life. This book sets out to help you see the invisible, so you can do the impossible. It will shine the light on the invisible inner walls created by trauma and give you the tools to begin dismantling them.

Perhaps you picked up this book because you're feeling trapped. You're feeling frustrated, enraged, burned out, dismissed, helpless, ashamed, anxious, depressed, lonely, fatigued, or sick.

Or perhaps you picked up this book because of what you're *not* feeling. Perhaps, despite checking off all the right boxes of career and motherhood and marriage, you are not feeling creatively, sexually, and professionally fulfilled, happy, peaceful, and comfortable in your skin.

Welcome to the sisterhood of jailbreakers.

ENTER PATRIARCHY STRESS DISORDER

When I started allowing the possibility that perhaps I, too, had trauma, the dots began to connect. When my dad yelled at me when I was a little girl, I would freeze and cry. When the last boss I had yelled at me, I would freeze and cry. Because the trauma of emotional abuse felt so familiar, it felt like "home," I never considered quitting. My "prison guards" made sure of that: the familiar equals safe. The prison guards generated stories in my mind, such as, "This is your dream job. It's prestigious.

Each time there's an opening for this position, there are hundreds of applicants. You'll never do better." If you were ever in an abusive relationship or know someone who was, understand that it's not the fault of the person being abused that they stay in them. Prison guards are the reason we stay. Trauma is the reason.

I also began to see some trauma symptoms and adaptations in women who didn't have trauma history in the conventional definition. These women came from very supportive families and did not recall any significant adverse experiences—emotional, physical, or sexual. As I was wondering about what these hidden traumas could possibly be, I kept seeing new scientific findings on intergenerational transmission of trauma, revealing that traumatic experiences get recorded and passed down in our DNA. More dots connected.

Women have been oppressed for millennia. Oppression is traumatic. If trauma is genetically transmitted, it may explain why women without any trauma history they could recall displayed trauma symptoms and adaptations.

This realization was really big. Not only does the invisible prison of trauma form through our own experiences—but we're born with the history of trauma and its adaptations, developed to keep us safe, imprinted in our DNA as a part of our survival instructions.

For women living under patriarchy, these survival instructions include: be seen and not heard, don't be too sexy, too loud, too smart, too rich, too visible, too powerful. Powerful women are burned at the stake. Or, as my mother used to warn me, "No one would want to marry you."

Once I saw this universal, collective trauma that all women share, I could not unsee it. Suddenly everything made sense. It made sense why no matter how much we achieve and how much personal growth work we do, women are still tormented by the inner critic and don't consistently *feel* good about ourselves. It made sense that even very successful women feel this way. Meryl Streep spoke about her imposter syndrome in an interview with Ken Burns: "You think, 'Why would anyone want to see me again in a movie? And I don't know how to act anyway, so why am I doing this?'"[2]

This discovery felt very important. It felt like the missing piece to the puzzle of not only creating the "good life" that we want, but also being able to enjoy it. It felt like the missing piece to stopping the war on ourselves, on our bodies. To getting off the hamster wheel of achievement and "self-improvement." To finally feeling happy and fulfilled, and comfortable in our skin, regardless of the circumstances.

Unless we recognize and learn the tools that can help heal this universal trauma, women are stuck trying to "break through" what's holding us back as if these were personal issues. They're not. *There's nothing wrong with*

---

2   Meryl Streep, interview by Ken Burns, *USA Weekend,* 2002.

you. Seeing the bigger picture of this shared trauma calls for solutions that involve healing it.

To help people see the invisible, I termed this insidious trauma, *Patriarchy Stress Disorder®* (PSD). Since the dots connected for me, I've shared my discovery with thousands of women via my podcast, newsletter, and live and virtual interviews and talks I gave at conferences and organizations across the country and internationally. (You can find these on my website, www.drvalerie.com.) The most common reaction was along these lines: "Thank God, somebody has put the words to what I've been feeling all my life, wondering what's wrong with me!"

This book will help you see this invisible trauma, its symptoms and effects, and the steps for healing it—so you can do the impossible (or what has always been impossible for a woman under patriarchy): be truly, unapologetically happy, free, fulfilled, and successful on your own terms.

WHAT THIS BOOK IS *REALLY* ABOUT

The discussion of the patriarchal culture and PSD is not a question of men versus women. Both the masculine and the feminine are severely traumatized in patriarchy's oppressive system. The cost of membership in patriarchy is that we must fit into very narrow definitions of gender and the roles and expectations that come with it, and this oppresses the authentic expression of everyone.

People along the gender spectrum experience this differently. Experiences of oppression based on race, sexual orientation, disability, socioeconomic status, and other characteristics form additional layers of trauma. This book is specific to women's experience, so that we may recognize how the trauma of patriarchal oppression affects us and heal our way to happiness and fulfillment. But it is my hope that it provides insights, tools, and strategies that benefit all humans. That it unites rather than divides. All humans have trauma, and this book is an invitation to uncover it and discover paths for healing it.

Women's happiness and fulfillment is the heartbeat of the book, but we can also look to a bigger view of the costs of the absence of trauma awareness from the cultural conversation and corporate world. This blind spot in advancing gender equality may have inadvertently contributed to skyrocketing burnout rates of high-achieving women and other painful unintended consequences on our health, relationships, and well-being. As a heartbreaking illustration of this point, the number of women CEOs of the Fortune 500 companies at the time of this writing is down 50 percent in just the past few months to less than 5 percent, with only *one* woman of color. Women's empowerment has gotten hijacked by the patriarchal overculture and became about giving a woman the "opportunity" to burn herself out by working harder and doing more while playing by the patriarchal rules. They used to burn us at the stake—now they just hand us the torches.

To end the epidemic of burnout and dissatisfaction among high-achieving women, we must see the invisible barriers to women's thriving in our work in the world, relationships, and health that are even more insidious than the external glass ceiling.

This book will make the invisible barriers visible by unpacking the trauma of oppression—how it's passed down between the generations, how it manifests and affects us, its costs to our lives, relationships, organizations, and society at large, and how it specifically affects women. I chose women as the largest historically oppressed group of people to which I also belong. My vision is that the information and the messages in this book serve every group of people who have been oppressed based on race, class, ability status, gender identity, and sexual orientation—as well as the allies. For many people whose membership in several historically oppressed groups creates layers of trauma complexity, I hope the information found in this book serves as validation of their journeys and conveys the message—*there's nothing wrong with you.*

The healing methodology described in this book can be used by people across the gender continuum. However, in every person's experience there's a lot of individual complexity. Please note that this book is not meant to diagnose or treat any health or mental health condition. Here, I offer insights from my own experiences and those of my clients. I highly recommend as you embark on your own healing journey, that you work with a mental health professional trained in mind-body trauma resolution. I've included my suggestions to help you find such a professional on my website.

This book is not a replacement for medical or psychological care; if you are experiencing symptoms that interfere with your daily life, seek a practitioner to help. This book may complement your work.

Nor is it a comprehensive deconstruction of the issues affecting women in society today. Since you're holding this book, you're already aware of these issues. It is my belief that social change goes hand-in-hand with personal healing. The latter is the focus of the book.

Outside experiences of oppression, every human has trauma—within a broad range of its variety, severity, and complexity. My hope is that this book serves everyone who reads it. That it helps you see the invisible inner walls that trauma has created in your relationships with yourself, your partners, family, coworkers, and people at large. That it helps you see yourself and others with more empathy and compassion. That it inspires you to get on the jailbreak journey and support others in theirs. That it begins a jailbreak movement to heal our relationships, organizations, and our culture—and create the world that supports everyone's happiness and fulfillment, authentic expression, safety, and thriving.

SCHEMING A JAILBREAK

This book details the plan for jailbreak. We'll begin with a tour of the prison of Patriarchy Stress Disorder—the ancestral, collective, and personal trauma of oppression—and you'll begin to see its walls.

Next, we'll meet what I call the "prison guards," the trauma adaptations that operate in us to keep us safe. You'll learn to recognize the guards, thank and befriend them, and evolve their job descriptions to become your "body guards"—so they can keep you safe not by keeping you locked up, but by protecting you on your journey to your deepest desires.

Then we'll begin to dig the tunnel to freedom. I'll show you how to safely work through the layers of individual, collective, and inherited trauma that are holding you back, and begin healing them and integrating the treasures that this excavation uncovers.

Once you've broken through to a life on the outside, there are no boxes to check off and no models to follow. You'll be charting new territory all on your own and reclaiming your relationship with your authentic desires as your guides and pleasure as your fuel.

In the final chapters, we'll take a look at how jailbreakers' lives, relationships, and work in the world change post-jailbreak.

We were all born into the prison of ancestral and collective trauma, designed by the patriarchal ethos. The deepest trauma women experience under patriarchy is that our lives, our bodies, and minds are not as valuable as men's. That we're worth *less*.

This core wound of worth-*less*-ness sets us up to check off the boxes of external achievement, only to have those achievements mask unhappiness and dis-ease—like putting up nice window treatments to cover the prison bars. You picked up this book because you've discovered that no matter how much success you create, you still feel like you are not enough. Now you know: it is not your fault or failure.

This book is for the woman who's done decorating the prison cell.

I love what you've done with the place. It's looking quite exquisite. You and I must have read the same prison cell decorating magazines. But now you're ready to experience the real thing—the vibrant colors, sensual textures, and titillating fragrances of your life on the outside. I'm thrilled you're joining me in jailbreak!

THE MISSING LINK

You have glimpsed the invisible prison walls somewhere in your life—in looking in the mirror and getting a sinking feeling at the sight of wrinkles and wondering if you should get a new "anti-aging" cream, Botox, or plastic surgery to keep time at bay. Or in tolerating the way your work environment does not see, care about, let alone encourage the full expression of your talents. Or in telling yourself that although you're not fully happy in your relationship, at least you have a partner. You diligently went to therapy, read self-help books, and attended personal development workshops and retreats—only to find yourself stuck on the hamster wheel of "self-improvement" turn after turn.

I saw this cycle in my clients long before I saw it in myself. Before the left side of my body pulled the emergency brake, I was stuck in my own hamster wheel—trying to outrun the pain of worth-*less*-ness by taking one personal development workshop after another, reading heaps of self-help books, while feverishly decorating my prison cell with more degrees, home remodeling, and diamonds for my wedding ring.

My left side was telling me the truth: I didn't feel *fully* alive. I was not living a whole life.

Soon after this realization, I felt intense grief. *What the hell happened to me? Who the hell was I before I got sucked into this hamster wheel? I can't remember.* I yearned to reclaim who I once was, to understand where I had lost myself and when I had become a dead woman walking.

I asked myself, what would bring me more pleasure and ease? If I could have everything my way, what would my life look like? My inner voice answered modestly at first. *I would take a lunch break. I would go pee when I want to pee, instead of holding it until I was done with my back-to-back clients. I would go outside. I would move my body every day.*

Then my inner voice got greedier: *I would shorten my fourteen-hour workdays. I would have more time off.* Each baby step led to a bigger step, my inner guidance leading me to make life-changing moves: *I would close my private practice and have location independence. I would expand the reach of my work from the therapy office to the world. I would share my message with millions of women. I would speak on stages, write a book, and work with conscious individuals and companies to create cultural shifts that would support people's success and thriving in every area of their lives.*

And so I listened and followed. The journey has taken me way beyond the invisible inner walls that enclosed the narrow perimeter of what I believed was possible for me. Not only in the outer circumstances, but in the way I feel inside. I wake up happy. Whack-a-mole addictions I used to numb the pain with—work, food, alcohol, stress, anger, and more—no longer shield me from being present in my life. I took up residence inside my body—a place that I rarely visited before, hanging out mostly in my head. I'm able to feel pleasure and joy so much deeper and navigate challenges with a lot more resilience.

My new life was born out of my deep authentic desires. Getting in touch with them took getting through the layers of prison guards. PSD makes sure they're well protected—there's nothing more dangerous to the patriarchal status quo than a woman who's in touch with her desires.

My mind resisted each one of them, screaming, *You*

cannot have that, because that doesn't exist! The voice of my desire replied, *Okay, maybe you're right. I'm just not going to settle for anything less.*

I relentlessly followed my joy. Over time, I have become a Rottweiler with my joy.

Throughout this book, I'll show you how to hold on to your joy, as though your life depends on it—because it does. Joy keeps you in touch with yourself and your desires. It's the True North of your life's journey. Joy is an essential elixir for your sex life and a potent "anti-aging" agent. Your health and well-being depend on it. So does your professional success and harmony in your relationships.

When I let my authentic desire drive, opportunities and relationships came into my life that were so much better than what my limited imagination could have ever conjured. In my work now, I get to share the teachings and techniques that have been responsible for my and my clients' transformations with people who are looking to break free from their own prisons. The desire that drives me now is that every woman knows her true beauty and her true power. And that she never trades them for the fake surrogate that patriarchy tries to sell to her at a very high price—of forgetting what a powerful and beautiful being she is.

This book was born of this desire.

CHAPTER ONE

WAKING UP IN PRISON

Our deepest fear is not that we are inadequate. Our deepest fear is that we are powerful beyond measure. It is our light, not our darkness, that most frightens us.

—MARIANNE WILLIAMSON

LESLIE WAS A RECOGNIZED EXPERT IN HER FIELD. She had a vision to pour her talents and experience into building her own business, so Leslie joined a mastermind. She invested tens of thousands of dollars to be in that room, knowing it would support her vision. After her presentation, another member approached her with an opportunity that fit her skillset and the direction she wanted to grow her business. He needed consultation around a new product line, and he wanted to pay Leslie for her guidance—to the tune of $350,000.

Weeks later, Leslie told me this part of the story, and

then quickly moved on to another topic. I stopped her and asked, "What happened with the offer?"

"What offer?"

"The consulting package that was offered to you."

Leslie was silent. She was processing. Eventually she asked again. "What do you mean?"

"Well, the entrepreneur who asked you to consult for him for $350,000. What did you do?"

She paused and took a deep breath. "I thanked him. And then I forgot about it." Leslie said. "I didn't follow up with him. I didn't do anything."

I realized that she had not considered the offer as a real possibility, so quickly had she dismissed that her skills and expertise could be so valuable to another person.

This is how trauma adaptations operate. Leslie's response to an offer that felt beyond her reach was to run away from it. In fact, she ran away while she was still in the room, still talking to that entrepreneur—she just checked out in her mind and disengaged completely, and later she forgot about it.

When trauma is triggered, it hijacks us out of the prefrontal cortex of the brain—our executive decision-making center, the seat of logic and reason—and drops us straight into the ancient hindbrain—focused on our survival—where words and notions don't exist. Certainly six-figure offers don't exist there. Leslie was so triggered that her prefrontal cortex barely registered the offer.

When triggered, a trauma response of fight, flight, or freeze gets activated to keep us safe. Leslie went into flight. It would be a great ending to this story to say that Leslie went back to the entrepreneur and took the offer. After our conversation, she did indeed reconnect with him, and his offer was still on the table. Ultimately, she declined it. The offer to be paid handsomely for her talents was an acknowledgment of her worth—which caused painful dissonance with her wound of worth-*less*-ness, so her mind created lots of "rational" stories to get her to move away from the discomfort. *He doesn't know me that well*, she thought. *He will be disappointed in me.* The work wasn't *exactly* in her area of expertise, she decided. Each of these stories was the bar of a jail cell to keep her safe. Familiar equals safe. Even if the familiar is a prison.

I can't help but wonder, had Leslie learned the jailbreak tools, if this story would have a different ending. We'll never know. But what we do know is that most people would do what Leslie did. They would choose the prison over jailbreak, the safety of the status quo over the risk of new experiences, even if very desirable. And they will justify this decision and believe their justification.

Consciously, Leslie thought of herself and showed up as a confident woman, aware and proud of her talents and accomplishments. But her subconscious imprinted a different story—the story of ancestral oppression based on gender, race, and social class, where a woman's power was a punishable offense.

No matter what we think, how much "mindset" work we do—the subconscious always wins. PSD wires it to sabotage our success and thriving to ensure our survival. Because survival is prioritized over success and thriving any day of the week.

As we'll see, this inner prison comes in many forms. Each with a very rational story that makes logical sense. There's a whole world outside that makes no sense at all, because it does not confirm the worth-*less*-ness wound of PSD—so the prison protects us from it.

THE PRISON FOUNDATIONS

The prison of PSD is built over a pit that is the original trauma inflicted upon women by patriarchy—the wound of worth-*less*-ness. The millennia of patriarchy have impressed upon us, beyond a shadow of a doubt, that women's bodies and minds are worth less than men's. The pain of this core wound is what we're trying to escape. We climb higher, and we build sophisticated scaffolding out of our careers, businesses, relationships, marriages, and families. We build up continuous achievements and milestones in our lives, but as we climb ever higher, we still don't gain freedom.

Then the scaffolding collapses.

We find ourselves in crisis: We have a huge blowout at work, or we find ourselves on the brink of divorce, or we wind up in the hospital. We tumble into the pit we worked so hard to avoid.

Most of my clients came to work with me after a part of their scaffolding collapsed. If we have the awareness, the support, the guidance, and the right tools—this is the perfect opportunity to dig the tunnel out of the prison. When we're on the prison floor, or have fallen through into the pit, we're so much closer to recognizing and healing the wound of worth-*less*-ness and reclaiming the treasures that make up our authenticity and wholeness that our traumas had shattered.

I classify these traumas as ancestral, collective, and individual. As we define those terms, you'll see that some of this trauma comes from personal events and experiences in your life that made you feel unsafe in your fullest authentic expression, while others were passed down to you from previous generations as survival instructions for a woman in a patriarchal culture.

Each trauma creates trauma adaptations—I refer to them as *prison guards*. Their job is to keep us safe. They accomplish it by keeping our bodies and minds in vigilant survival mode, despite our best efforts to thrive. Jailbreak is possible when we start to notice how these adaptations show up in our lives, when we understand the need for safety they are serving, and we create the experience of safety necessary for the prison guards to allow—and actually support—our safe passage to freedom.

Before we can dig, we must take a look around at exactly where we are. In the first step of your jailbreak, I invite you to explore what your own prison is made of.

ANCESTRAL TRAUMA

The invisible inner prison was not built in your lifetime. You were born into it. The first layer of trauma that created it is likely to have been passed down to you in the DNA.

The new science of epigenetics has shown us that gene expression can and does change in response to environmental changes and experiences, and that these changes are inheritable. Increasingly, studies are showing that trauma adaptations can be genetically transmitted across generations as a part of our survival instructions.

A review of studies on combat soldiers with PTSD showed that their traumatic experiences had resulted in epigenetic changes that could be inherited by their offspring.[3] Another study of women who were pregnant during the Tutsi genocide in Rwanda found that their children had inherited trauma-induced epigenetic changes.[4] Other studies found that the children of Holocaust survivors had inherited traits associated with the stress response of their parents.[5]

An even more fascinating experiment on mice found

---

3   Nagy A. Youssef, Laura Lockwood, Shaoyong Su, Guang Hao, Bart P.F. Rutten, "The Effects of Trauma, with or without PTSD, on the Transgenerational DNA Methylation Alterations in Human Offsprings," *Brain Sciences*, 2018, 8(5): 83.

4   N. Perroud, E. Rutembesa, A. Paoloni-Giacobino, J. Mutabaruka, L. Mutesa, L. Stenz, A. Malafosse, and F. Karege, "The Tutsi Genocide and Transgenerational Transmission of Maternal Stress," *Biological Psychiatry*, May 2014, 15(4):334-45.

5   Rachel Yehuda, Nikolaos P. Daskalakis, Linda M. Bierer, Heather N. Bader, Torsten Klengel, Florian Holsboer, and Elisabeth B. Binder, "Holocaust Exposure Induced Intergenerational Effects on *FKBP5* Methylation," *Biological Psychiatry*, September 1, 2016, 80(5):372-380.

that subsequent generations could be made to inherit trauma not in response to genocide or war, but to mild electric shocks paired with the smell of cherry blossoms.[6] Researchers piped the smell of cherry blossoms into the cages of mice, and simultaneously, they zapped the mice's feet with mild electric shocks. This conditioned the mice to have a stress response to the smell. They were then bred, and the offspring were raised without being exposed to the smell of cherry blossoms.

A look into the mice's heads showed that the offspring had more neurons devoted to detecting cherry blossom smell in their brains and noses. When they were exposed to the smell, the offspring became anxious and fearful. The mice were bred again, and the smell of cherry blossoms elicited the same fear and anxiety reaction in the grandchildren of the traumatized mice. Neuroscientists discovered that epigenetic markers transmitted a traumatic experience across generations, shaping their behavior according to the trauma adaptations.

PSD is women fearing the smell of cherry blossoms. Being unapologetically visible, authentically expressing our brilliance and sexuality, being in touch with our desires and going after them—showing up in our power is the smell of cherry blossoms that we were taught to fear through the trauma of oppression that has spanned countless generations.

---

6   Meeri Kim, "Study Finds that Fear can Travel Quickly through Generations of Mice DNA," *The Washington Post,* December 7, 2013.

A woman's power has always been a punishable offense. Under patriarchy, it's never been safe for a woman to be visible. For the crime of being visible in their power, women used to be burned at the stake, drowned, and beheaded. We may not have directly been persecuted for our power, but we came from the generations of women before us who have been traumatically conditioned not to reach for the cherry blossoms—because they were either dangerous or unattainable.

Patriarchal oppression of women through legislature and social norms that control women's bodies, voices, and money isn't all ancient history. In the US, until the Women's Business Ownership Act of 1988, a woman could not take out a business loan without a signature of a male relative. Women's rights—around voting, educational and employment opportunities, birth control, abortion, divorce, protection from marital rape and from sexual harassment in the workplace—have only been established within the last 100 years, most much more recently than that.

Most shifts toward gender parity have taken place within two or three most recent generations. If humans are at least as connected with their parents and grandparents as mice, we can appreciate the stress that the smell of cherry blossoms—of opportunities—creates for women. In addition to the epigenetic mechanisms of trauma transmission we've seen in mice, humans have storytelling, familial, and cultural programming. And unlike our traumatized mice friends, generation after generation, women continue to get re-traumatized. Women's rights are still facing strong headwinds from the patriarchal status quo today.

This trauma doesn't just dissolve as external conditions change. For the mice who never experienced the electric shocks, the smell of cherry blossoms still caused distress. The survival instructions in our DNA dictate what we must—and must not—do to protect ourselves. Each instruction, based on another layer of trauma, narrows our subconscious sense of what is possible. It makes our invisible inner prison cell smaller.

Ancestral trauma does not spring from the events in our own lives, and yet we carry it with us and pass it along to the next generations—until we heal it. This trauma does not "belong to us" individually, but it shapes how each one of us shows up in the world today. When we heal it, we end the cycle of trauma transmission, liberating not only ourselves, but the future generations.

Based on ancestral trauma, our subconscious has been programmed to protect us from being too successful, powerful, wealthy, or happy. Our subconscious has imprinted survival instructions along these lines. We must be seen and not heard. We must be attractive—enough to be accepted, but not too attractive—lest we won't be taken seriously. We mustn't go for that promotion, or we won't be liked. We mustn't be too smart, or no man will want to date or marry us. We mustn't be too sexy, or we'll be raped. We mustn't shine too brightly and draw attention, or we'll be in danger of persecution.

Now, consciously, you probably don't believe any of these patriarchal precepts. But it's your subconscious that calls the shots. Neuroscientists have found that almost all our decisions are made in the subconscious—with the conscious mind merely stepping in to rationalize them (more fascinating studies are coming out all the time; we keep collecting them for your reference on my website). Our subconscious is rooted in survival. And it operates according to the survival instructions. Survival takes precedence over thriving any day of the week. Subconscious always wins.

This is a very brief summary of science that debunks the harmful self-help postulate that sells a lot of "self-improvement" hamster wheels—that you're "holding yourself back." *You're not.* Generation after generation, you were taught to fear the smell of cherry blossoms. Once we understand how these messages and instructions are created, transmitted, and how they affect us, we can learn to create the healing conditions to resolve intergenerational trauma. As we resolve trauma, we can have our subconscious support our dreams—not sabotage them, in order to keep us safe. We can map out our jailbreak.

COLLECTIVE TRAUMA

The first hold of trauma comes from the disempowerment and persecution of our ancestors, but the second method by which trauma keeps a hold on us is through collective experiences of women today.

Around the globe, women are subjected to genital mutilation, child marriage, sexual violence, barriers to education, and severe economic disempowerment. In Saudi Arabia, a major US economic partner, women got to vote for the first time in 2015 and got to drive in 2018. Each time we turn on the television or tune in to social media, we are made aware of the collective state of women in the world. These stories trigger the original wound of PSD—the wound of being worth *less*.

Although in the US women enjoy a lot more rights and freedoms, our worth-*less*-ness is communicated to us through financial and political inequities, as well as social norms. In the workplace, the wage gap persists. According to a 2019 National Partnership for Women and Families report on the gender and ethnicity wage gap, Latinas are paid 53 cents for every dollar paid to white, non-Hispanic men. Native American women are paid 58 cents on the dollar, Black women 61 cents, White, non-Hispanic women 77 cents, and Asian women 85 cents.[7] In the entrepreneurial arena, women also face economic disadvantages. According to an article in *Fortune*, in 2018

---

7   "Quantifying America's Gender Wage Gap by Race/Ethnicity," *National Partnership for Women and Families,* April 2019.

women founders received only 2.2% of venture capital dollars.[8]

At the time of this writing, the US laws continue to control the female body by regulating abortion access, whereas there aren't any laws that allow the government to regulate the male body. These laws are created primarily by men. Representation of women, particularly women of color, although on the rise, is still far from parity.

The war on women waged by the patriarchal culture expresses in social norms that rank women's conditional worth on the basis of such characteristics as skin color, age, weight, body shape, and "feminine" traits.

As a result, PSD expresses not only in the constant stress from the external factors that police our authentic expression, dictate our worth, and limit our access to political and financial power. An even more insidious expression is the war on women that it is internalized—in the ways in which the "prison guards" in the invisible inner prison of trauma police our own authentic expression, dictate our worth, and limit our opportunities.

PSD created a blueprint of worth-*less*-ness in our subconscious, which makes it challenging to engage in experiences that affirm our worth—be it in relationships or business arenas.

Leslie's story is a typical example of how this plays

---

8   Emma Hinchliffe, "Funding for Female Founders Stalled at 2.2% of VC Dollars in 2018," *Fortune*, January 28, 2019.

out: We automatically dismiss anything that is not consistent with our subconscious sense of our worth. Just think of yourself receiving compliments. Do you dodge them? Hastily return them? Or do you actually *receive* them as an accurate, appropriate, and welcome reflection of your beauty and power?

The challenge with receiving limits the reach and impact of a woman's work in the world, the growth of her bank accounts, and the intimacy and pleasure in her partnerships. Women commonly self-sabotage good things that carry with them a reflection of their worth—because it's *dissonant* with the trauma of worth-*less*-ness. In Leslie's case—and in so many others—trying to imagine that her expertise could be compensated at such a high level created cognitive dissonance in her mind. So she ran.

Warren Buffett spoke to this cultural conditioning in the documentary *Becoming Warren Buffett*. "My sisters are fully as smart as I am," he said, "they got better personalities than I have, but they got the message that their future was limited and I got the message that the sky is the limit. It was the culture."[9]

The unconscious privilege of men under patriarchy is being believed in. They are born into the culture where they see 95 percent of Fortune 500 companies are run by men, the country where 100 percent of presidents at the time of this writing have been male. No matter what pretty words about women's empowerment are placed

9   Peter W. Kunhardt, dir, *Becoming Warren Buffett,* 2017; Pleasantville, NY: Kunhardt Films.

in commencement speeches and social media memes, as long as women don't see themselves represented in places of power, the message we receive and imprint is: you're worth *less*.

A particular study[10] illustrates how early these messages affect us. In the study, groups of five-, six- and seven-year-olds were read stories wherein the main character was described as "really, really smart."

"This person figures out how to do things quickly," the reader said, "and comes up with answers much faster and better than anyone else. This person is really, really smart." The stories didn't reveal the gender of the main character.

At age five, both boys and girls were likely to associate the gender of the main character with their own gender. But by age six or seven, just as these children were beginning to get socialized in school, the girls overwhelmingly identified the gender of the main character as male. The societal stereotype that views brilliance as a male trait has already been imprinted on them.

This research is not from the 1950s—this study was published in 2017.

Another study uncovered that when a woman experienced an objectifying gaze from a man for a few seconds before taking a math test, her performance was nega-

10 Lin Bian, Sarah-Jane Leslie, and Andrei Cimpian, "Gender Stereotypes about Intellectual Ability Emerge Early and Influence Children's Interests," *Science,* January 27, 2017, 355(6323): 389-391.

tively affected. The study found no negative effects on a man's performance following experiencing an objectifying gaze from a female.[11]

Given the wide-spread nature of this experience for women—the ongoing cultural trauma of objectification—I believe this study gives us but a glimpse into its far-ranging consequences for women's professional performance, mental health, and wellness.

The cultural trauma of conscious and unconscious gender bias across professional fields is another uphill battle that takes a toll on women's productivity, creativity, and well-being day in and day out. An engineer described a time when she submitted a presentation to her boss. The only feedback he had did not have to do with the content. "You'll need to change the colors on the deck," he said. "*Pink* is not an engineering color."

This communication expressed his unconscious gender bias: women can't be engineers—don't remind us that you're a woman.

Over time, women develop layers of trauma adaptations to protect ourselves against cultural trauma. They help us tolerate hostile environments. Because we've learned that tolerating hostile environments is necessary for success under patriarchy. Common adaptations among successful women include chronic high stress levels, workaholism, and unconsciously shaping our

---

11 Sarah J. Gervais, Theresa K. Vescio, and Jill Allen, "When What You See Is What You Get," *Psychology of Women Quarterly*, January 25, 2011, 35(1): 5-17.

ways of thinking, acting, and being to be more like men. Predictably, these go hand-in-hand with issues with sleep and weight, adrenals and thyroid, female organs such as breasts and the reproductive system, anxiety, depression, and addictions. Parenting problems, strained relationships with children and partners, dead or unsatisfying sex lives, prescription meds to mask the symptoms and their side effects are so disturbingly common—they are an expected "price of success" among high-achieving women.

The staggering cost of the trauma adaptations associated with PSD is the deadening effect they have on our lives: the disconnection they create from our true authentic essence, making us forget, leave behind parts of who we truly are. Because these parts don't fit in the patriarchal prison, they end up being edited out from our authentic wholeness—just like the color pink from the engineering deck.

INDIVIDUAL TRAUMA

The American Psychological Association defines trauma as an emotional response "to a terrible event like an accident, rape or natural disaster."[12] It also recognizes adverse childhood experiences (ACEs) as traumatic. These include physical, sexual, and emotional abuse; physical and emotional neglect; exposure to adult incar-

---

12 "Trauma," *American Psychological Association*, 2019.

ceration, mental illness, substance abuse, or violence in the household; parental separation or divorce; poverty, bullying, exposure to community violence, and discrimination.[13]

The definition I offered earlier captures an even broader experience: *trauma is any event or circumstance that made you feel unsafe in your fullest authentic expression and resulted in creating trauma adaptations.*

None of us escapes the experience of being shut down by others, ignored, yelled at, or criticized. Growing up in a home where a parent is depressed or has their own stressors can create an environment in which we feel unsafe in our fullest authentic expression. The trauma adaptations may look like withdrawing and making ourselves smaller to protect ourselves from experiencing the pain of rejection or criticism, or feeling unwanted.

Many of my clients, when they first come to me, believe they have not experienced trauma. They explain that they had great childhoods, full of great memories. When we begin our work and begin digging together, we discover experiences that made them feel shut down, ignored, or unsafe in some way.

Each of these experiences is a knot in a web that holds them back.

Even experiences that we consider insignificant or normal can define our thoughts, behaviors, and choices.

---

13   Sharon G. Portwood, "Adverse Childhood Experiences," *American Psychological Association*, November 2018.

These are mild electric shocks we received while reaching for cherry blossoms. We do not easily think of these experiences as trauma because they are commonplace and seemingly benign. That's just life. But life, as it turns out, includes great deals of trauma, and when we become aware of these experiences, each one presents an opportunity to heal.

Sometimes my clients come to me aware of the traumatic experiences they've had, but they believe that they're "over it," they've "dealt with it," they've "worked through it"—because they talked about it in therapy before. But talking about a traumatic experience does not resolve trauma. These experiences are lodged in our bodies. They are imprinted in the nervous system reactions that got wired to that event or experience.

The body remembers feeling unsafe. And it reminds us each time this trauma gets triggered. The mind may create stories, explanations, and rationalizations. But the body never lies.

In our jailbreak, we'll engage the body's wisdom, memory, and intelligence to guide us to freedom through trauma healing.

THE PRISON SECURITY SYSTEM

Just as post-traumatic stress disorder develops in the wake of a trauma, PSD comprises layers of ancestral trauma, in combination with the collective feminine trauma and the individual trauma we experience in a world where it's never been safe to be a woman.

It's important to know that what hurts us in the present moment is not the trauma itself; it's our trauma adaptations—the defenses we developed in response to our inherited, collective, and individual traumatic experiences. Some of these adaptations are our daily companions, e.g., high stress levels that are keeping the nervous system in a state of constant hypervigilance—ready to fight or flee to keep us safe. Others get activated when trauma is triggered—such as, when an upcoming public speaking opportunity resonates with the ancestral, collective, or personal wounds around visibility and speaking one's mind. These adaptations may include procrastination, anxiety, and various forms of self-sabotage meant to protect us from danger.

I call these defenses our "prison guards." While their job is to keep us safe, they do so by locking us in survival, at the expense of our thriving. The guards tell us that it is safer on the inside, within the confines of our history of oppression.

Our *minds, bodies,* and *actions* cooperate to maintain this safety.

Our minds create whatever stories will keep us from breaking out of jail. These are our self-defeating stories, our stories about self-doubt, confidence, and self-esteem (or lack thereof), and imposter syndrome. "Who do you think you are?" "You're a fraud." "This will never work."

Our mind tells us these stories to keep us from reaching our goals, dreams, and desires—because doing so would get us out of the safety of the certainty of the PSD prison and into the dangerous world outside.

Another layer of the prison security system lies in the action domain. The prison guards here manifest as distractions, procrastination, being frozen in inaction, or engaging in various kinds of self-sabotage. Addictive behaviors fall into this category too—overeating, overworking, overdrinking, overshopping, overexercising, or drowning in streaming shows. These actions also keep us safely imprisoned.

Mindset work will not help us jailbreak. Many personal growth seminars, empowerment programs, and self-help books urge us to think positively, say affirmations, and jump into action. These popular approaches advocate that we push through our defenses. If we can just change our mindset, they tell us, we can do anything.

But these approaches ignore one very important fact. Our defenses are there for a reason. That reason being self-preservation, survival, and safety.

If the defenses on the level of the mind or action fail, survival needs to be ensured by other means. Our defense system is very sophisticated.

We may change the way we think, but the prison guards will sound the alarm. *There's been a security breach! We need reinforcements!* More prison guards will come rushing in.

The more defenses we push through, the more costly it is to our nervous system. The prison guards show up on the level of the body as health expressions, anxiety, depression, adrenal fatigue, trouble sleeping, and stress addiction—inability to slow down or stop and relax. The stories that we believe we're combatting within the mind alone become somaticized: they manifest in a wide array of stress responses in the body.

For high-achieving women, it's usually our health that breaks. We push through the defenses on the level of the mind and action—*self-doubt, self-schmout, I'm just going to do it, okay?* Many coaching and "personal growth" approaches advocate treating fear as the enemy and pushing through it to break through. Many high-achieving women follow these misguided strategies and push through—until their adrenals blow out—and break through—until their health falls apart. A host of symptoms floods in, ranging from fatigue to hormone imbalances to autoimmune issues.

Stress-related conditions and trauma are directly connected. Stress is a trauma adaptation for the nervous system, keeping us in a state of hypervigilance and hyper-activation to make sure we're always aware of unsafe conditions that surround us. What's more, we often don't even feel we're stressed: because we were born in the prison, we've inherited this trauma adaptation. High stress feels normal until our health begins to crack.

We have to put out the torches they've handed us! In

the subsequent chapters I'll show you, step-by-step, how to do it safely and effectively—without sacrificing, but in fact getting back more of your time and productivity.

HOW OUR BODIES REACT TO UNSAFE EXPERIENCES

Our bodies react to threats with a fight, flight, or freeze response. When we experience trauma, whether on an individual or collective level, our system files the experience under "threats." When an aspect of another situation has the flavor of that threat (something in it looks, sounds, smells, tastes, feels similar)—our survival instincts are triggered, our nervous system activates, and we are sent once again into fight, flight, or freeze.

We are not always consciously aware of what feels threatening to our system. Walking down the street or taking a taxi can put us on guard. We look over our shoulders. We brace ourselves as we turn on the TV, where the news ranges from kidnappings, rapes, and murders of women, to debates about women's rights, to beauty propaganda that polices women's bodies.

Feeling unsafe inside our own bodies or in the outside world is a woman's baseline. As a result, our nervous systems stay in a high level of activation—which translates into chronic stress and can lead to chronic illness.

TRACKING OUR REACTIONS

The mind explains what the body experiences. Our thoughts don't come first; our body sensations do. The mind plays catch-up and makes sense and meaning out of what we felt.

Imagine that a ball has been thrown at you. You don't see it coming, but you instinctively turn to it and catch it. Your action comes first, and then your mind explains what just happened. "This is a ball. It came from over there. Somebody must be playing catch." Your body reacts first, and your mind explains later.

When your body is in fight, your mind constructs a story that justifies and fans the fire of that state. Since this state was originally triggered for self-preservation, your mind takes the ball and runs with it. One of the best ways your mind can support this state is to tell you a story that agitates you. For example, in an argument with your husband, your mind might say: *It's his fault. He's always putting himself first. He never listens to me. He's probably having an affair.* In fight mode, your mind eggs you on. It instigates.

The stories our minds tell in flight are stories of disengagement. For example, when dealing with your finances—an uncomfortable area for many women—you might not even look at your bank account. Overwhelmed by all the money coming in and coming out, your mind might generate stories like: *I'm going to do it later. I'm not good at spreadsheets.*

When your body experiences freeze, the mind explains the experience with a story that supports freeze. It will tell you: *Don't do this—you're going to fail anyway. It makes no sense.*

Let's take a look at two all-too-common conditions that arise from chronic nervous system activation.

ANXIETY AND DEPRESSION

Anxiety is like a rattling lid on the boiling pot of your authentic desires. The lid has been put there and secured by PSD, and it's been there so long you don't even know what's inside the pot. Sometimes you catch a delicious whiff from underneath the lid. Which, just like the smell of cherry blossoms, feels dangerous. And the lid gets secured tighter.

The lid's rattling—that's what you're aware of as *the problem*. It agitates you. You just want it to stop. Rather than lifting the lid to look inside, you focus on getting rid of the annoying sound. This is anxiety.

Anxiety is connected to the fight and flight reactions of the nervous system, and it is a state of hypervigilance. It's meant to protect us by constantly anticipating danger. These reactions urge us to action: we have the impulse to fight or flee bubbling up, but the lid stifles our response.

Depression is connected to the freeze reaction. This chronic freeze state is a trauma adaptation that our bodies engage to deal with the high levels of chronic activation. It numbs us out from our pain.

Depression is also a state of apathy. It starts as a trauma defense to protect us from the perceived impossibilities of our desires and our dreams. Depression starts with an activating event—something that leaves us heartbroken, disappointed, or in grief—and then it takes on a life of its own. We get stuck in sadness, and apathy sets in to unplug us from the pain. In depression we can't bring ourselves to act, and therefore it keeps us safe from being hurt again.

Though we may very much want to get out of the painful state of depression, part of us feels comforted by the paralysis.

While depressed, we have difficulty summoning energy. Our body feels heavy and lethargic. Our thoughts reinforce this state. *What's the use of getting out of bed? Why bother?*

This is what trauma does. It unplugs us from our life force. It turns our emotions and our desires into unsafe places to go.

These two expressions, anxiety and depression, stem from the activity of our prison guards that are keeping us "safely" imprisoned—with agitation in anxiety and apathy in depression.

Both conditions signal our disconnection from our true desires. This is a big outcome of the trauma of PSD: it dictates what is safe and what is not, and it creates an environment in which we don't let ourselves truly go there—to the heart of our own desires.

JOURNALING
WHAT ARE YOU TOLERATING?

It can be difficult to see all the ways the different forms of trauma operate in our lives because often those patterns are so ingrained. One of our biggest clues is in the parts of our lives that we're tolerating. What circumstances in your life pinch just a little? What are you putting up with, and why? Take a few minutes to reflect. In your answers you'll begin to see the outline of the prison walls.

WHAT IS YOUR DEEPEST DESIRE?

The prison guards know: there is really nothing more dangerous to patriarchy than a woman who is in touch with her desires. As a consequence, the prison guards protect you from connecting with your deepest desire. Within the supplemental materials at www.drvalerie.com, you can find a guided meditation on connecting with your desire.

As you listen to the meditation, notice what gets in the way of that connection. Those are your prison guards: Say hello to them and recognize that they are there to keep you safe. We'll work with them throughout this book.

After the meditation, journal about any breadcrumbs you have discovered to lead you to your desire. Don't censor yourself, and don't edit anything out. Nothing is silly or outrageous.

Journal about any prison guards that jumped in to block you from knowing your true desire, for example, through stories or distractions.

You may discover when you try to connect with your desire that nothing comes up—and this too is a win. It provides helpful information about your prison guards: it may mean that your desire feels so big and so dangerous that it is very well-protected. As you go through this book, we'll learn to work with the prison guards, and I encourage you to return to this meditation on an ongoing basis. Notice how your experience changes. Each prison guard you notice protecting your desire, and each breadcrumb you find leading you closer to your desire, is a big win.

TOUCHING JOY, TOUCHING PAIN

In the fifteen years that I worked as a psychotherapist, I've noticed that underlying every condition—from depression to anxiety, to problems with addiction, relationships, and self-esteem—there was some kind of trauma.

In the long run, it is not the *trauma* that hurts us, but the defenses, the adaptations, the complex mechanisms we develop that protect us from touching it again. These same mechanisms protect us from feeling joy, ecstasy, happiness, fulfillment, and pleasure. Because our capacity to feel pleasure, joy, and fulfillment equals our capacity to feel grief, loss, and sadness.

As we saw before, these protective mechanisms ensure our safety, and we cannot simply override them. If we try to override them, something else will backfire in the system. Real change does not happen when these defenders are activated. The only way to create lasting change is to establish safety and allow the prison guards to step down from their duties.

We can help the prison guards evolve into bodyguards by using tools grounded in psychology, biology, and neuroscience to create embodied safety. When we're able to do that, the guards' job description changes: instead of keeping us safe by keeping us locked up, they now protect us on the journey of growth and change, making it possible for us to create and experience what we desire in our lives—and feel safe along the way.

The jailbreak system came out of my own healing journey, where I was fortunate to study with many pioneers of mind-body approaches to mental health, healing, and trauma resolution.

THE POWER OF EMBODIMENT

By the time I made it into the master's program at Columbia University, I had suffered two episodes of major depression. Statistically speaking, I had an 80 percent likelihood of relapse within five years. I was afraid that my depression would be a life sentence.

I was in a program for psychological counseling and

struggling with incapacitating anxiety and panic attacks. Each time I would raise my hand in class, I broke into a sweat, my heart raced, my thoughts would leave my mind, and I would leave my body.

Of course, I was in therapy. It helped me gain insight, but it didn't help alleviate my symptoms in any way. Which made matters worse. Yes, it was nice to share my problems with a therapist for forty-five minutes once a week. But the fact that here I was, training to become a therapist, seeing a therapist week after week and not getting any better, made me feel like a complete failure.

Working out made me feel marginally better. At the time, the scaffolding I was focused on building within my PSD jail cell was all about how I looked and how much I weighed. I gave myself some conditional approval based on how well I could maintain my weight under the 122-pound cut-off line. One day, I was on the elliptical, observing through the glass wall of the exercise studio in front of me a yoga class. I'd never taken one and I was intrigued. All those size-zero girls doing all these crazy bendy things, looking so sexy. I wanted to do that. I wanted to be that. So I went to my first yoga class.

And after a few minutes, I rushed out, panicked.

It turned out, I was not able to hold a pose for five breaths. The poses weren't difficult. Physically, I could do them—but my mind was racing. Each pose was an invitation to be in my body, but trying to be in my body, following my breath, created panic. It did not feel safe. I had to get out of there.

But I went back. The sexy bendy size-zero girls that I wanted to be, or the challenge, or my intuition got me back on the mat. I got through more of the class before walking out.

I repeated that again. And again. Until one day, I got through the entire class and landed in the final relaxation pose, *savasana*. I felt so deeply relaxed like I've never felt before. It was an entirely new experience—feeling safe and secure in my body. I wanted more of that. So much so that soon after, I completed a yoga teacher training program.

With a regular practice of yoga, to which I later added specific embodied trauma resolution tools, my anxiety resolved, and I haven't had a depression relapse in twenty years—without therapy or medication.

Coming back into my body, making my body my friend and a safe place to be, took time. But even the realization that I had not lived in my body in years was a pivotal moment on my healing journey.

What does embodiment feel like?

Remember your best vacation? Perhaps you went to the beach, and you felt the sand between your toes. You could smell the details of the ocean: the salt and seaweed and slippery fish. You heard the waves, one rolling after another, the fidelity of their crashing. Through your senses, you were uniquely connected to everything around you. You felt everything in you.

Imagine feeling this level of sensation and connection throughout your day, long after you've left the beach and returned home. That is embodiment: awareness of your sensory environment and the inner movements of your emotions.

At the start of my journey into embodiment, I realized that I hadn't felt that way in years. There was something dead about me, something robotic, that kept me from fully showing up. Trauma makes it feel unsafe to be in the body, and the head is a great place to hide.

When did I last feel fully alive? I was nineteen. I was a free spirit in how I dressed and expressed myself. I felt unencumbered, unconcerned with conforming. A sense of adventure and openness to the world were driving me to take opportunities. I was creative, I wrote a lot of poetry. My authentic self took up a whole lot of the space inside me.

Why nineteen? I thought. Why is that the last time I remember feeling alive?

At nineteen, I had my first sexual trauma. I had sex when I didn't want to. He used manipulation, coercion. It was effective. To go through with it, I had to turn off parts of myself. I had to disembody. I had to leave the unsafe place that my body has become and take refuge in my head. It was like taking a bite of the poisoned apple and falling asleep.

I talked about this experience with multiple therapists, while remaining disembodied, firmly planted in my head.

In all fairness, disembodiment is a norm in our society. And for disembodied therapists who haven't done their own trauma healing work it's not something they would recognize or would know what to do with.

That yoga class began a long journey of studying with the pioneers of mind-body trauma healing, relearning to live embodied, to feel safe, vital, and happy, anxiety- and depression-free in my body, enjoy deep intimate relationships, and pour my energy and talents into rewarding work in the world. In this book, I want to share with you what I've discovered on my journey about the nature of the trauma imprisonment and how to free yourself. I want you to experience your true power.

This power does not come from forcing yourself to push through your defenses. This power comes from recognizing the invisible inner prison, connecting with your desires, and cultivating the internal safety to jailbreak from the confines of old traumas and into embodied, empowered life on the outside.

CHAPTER TWO

———

MEET THE PRISON GUARDS

Trauma makes us less shiny and causes us to take up less space...It's like putting your whole life in Spanx.

—BERNADETTE PLEASANT, HER SUCCESS
RADIO PODCAST INTERVIEW

ELEANOR'S HUSBAND CAME TO SEE ME FIRST. IT'S rare for the man in the heterosexual relationship to initiate counseling, but Keith was concerned because although he loved his wife and knew she loved him, there was a big rift of alienation between them that he couldn't quite understand.

They had done all the things they were supposed to do: they'd moved from the city to the suburbs and bought a big house to have a family in. Yet every time Keith brought up the subject of having children, Eleanor would freeze up. She refused to engage.

When she came in to talk about it, Eleanor voiced

that she wanted to have children but it really scared her. All her friends were having kids, and she was feeling more isolated, more entrenched in her private pain: torn between wanting to be a mother and petrified at the possibility. She felt stuck. She felt frozen. Keith felt helpless. They were becoming more and more isolated in their relationship and from each other.

Eleanor was stuck at work, too. She was a talented professional, but felt her talents were being stifled. Management refused to give her the creative freedom and trust she needed to implement her vision. On top of that, she was having difficulties with her coworkers.

She had a regular habit to cope with her pain—something her family had done for generations—which was to unwind with some wine at the end of the day. Every night she would have a couple of glasses of wine, maybe more. It was a daily ritual to numb the pain.

It also numbed her desires at work and in her relationship.

Drinking was a great mechanism to cope with these problems, because it made some things impossible, like motherhood. Eleanor was a responsible woman. She would not consider getting pregnant while she was dependent on alcohol. The drinking was multipurpose: it numbed her pain and kept her choice at bay.

Eleanor was becoming more and more moody. The more she drank, the more isolated she felt. She didn't drink for pleasure or connection; she drank for numbness.

Her desires felt too painful, so she drank to disconnect from them.

But Eleanor and Keith didn't come to me to work on the drinking. They came to me specifically to understand her ambivalence about motherhood and the lack of intimacy they were having in their relationship. It worried both of them. Keith was supportive, and in one session he said to Eleanor, "If it's true for you—if you really, genuinely don't want to have children, it will not affect our relationship. I'm in full support of what feels right and authentic to you."

The problem was, she was not able to say what felt right and authentic to her. She had been disconnecting from her feelings for long enough that she didn't feel entitled to her genuine desires. She felt pressure, now that she was married, to want motherhood, but she simply didn't know if it was the right path for her. She continued to drink to avoid solving what felt so unsolvable to her.

They speak of my drinking, the Scottish proverb goes, *but never of my thirst.*

I wanted to know about her thirst.

Pain and desire can go hand and hand. Pain stems from needs that are not being fulfilled, and the attendant fear that they will never be fulfilled. *So why go there? Let's just disconnect.* But going into the pain can unlock the desire behind it.

It soon became very obvious that for Eleanor to go there, she had to be able to stay with herself in the here and now. She needed to be able to keep her attention present long enough to connect with herself. She was having a lot of trouble doing that. In conversation, her defenses were so elaborate and well trained. In parts of our conversations she presented as her adult self: articulate, intelligent, brilliant. In her discomfort she would shift, and she sounded and acted like a five-year-old: being cute, adorably forgetting what we just talked about, feeling flustered and uncomfortable.

Through these signs I recognized that Eleanor was likely to have experienced trauma around that age. But she wasn't ready to go there yet. She didn't have capacity. She was having difficulty holding her attention in her body in the present to help develop that ability. I recommended that she start taking yoga classes.

She came back the following week, sat down, looked me in the eye, and blurted, "Here is why I'm not going to take yoga."

She reached into her purse and pulled out a flyer. On the flyer was a photo of a size-zero girl, upside down, her body pretzeled in Scorpion pose. Eleanor was a curvy woman, and felt her very existence was shamed by that flyer.

I thanked her for sharing that with me. I told her the story of how I walked out of my first yoga class, and my second, and my third. I encouraged her to find a different studio that did not have those fliers, and to go to a restorative, therapeutic, or beginner class. I suggested she put her mat right by the door so she could leave at any point she wanted. She could even tell the teacher it was her first class and she may need to walk out if it became too much. These steps, I knew, would create the safety Eleanor needed.

She found a studio with wonderful teachers, where she felt comfortable. She started practicing regularly and using the tools I was teaching her in our sessions to create embodied safety.

Little by little, Eleanor built up capacity to process childhood trauma—which she hadn't realized she had. Trauma healing opened up even more capacity to connect with herself and her desires and engage in challenging conversations about them. As she dug deeper, it became very obvious to her that her drinking was blocking her from having what she wanted.

Addiction doesn't just go away because we want it to, however.

When Eleanor expressed her desire to quit drinking, her fear was so powerful that she was shaking all over in a full-body panic. She was about to give up the security blanket that had been helping her mask her anxiety, helping her deal with her pain, and made her bulletproof to failure by holding her back from pursuing her dreams. We had previously had conversations about rehab. Eleanor was worried she wouldn't be able to follow through with it. If she were to give up drinking, then what?

Keith sat beside her during this session. I asked Eleanor, "Do you trust this man?"

He had been there for her entire journey. He wasn't judging her. He was supporting any choice she wanted to make.

"Yes," she said.

"This is the time when you outsource your free will to him and allow him to take you to rehab."

Eleanor allowed herself to let go of control. She did her work at rehab, came back, and continued using the tools we'd been working on. Her integration was beautiful, and she and Keith worked through it together. She was able to replace the old security blanket of drinking with healthy, supportive behaviors like yoga and exercise. Eleanor and Keith went on walks and cooked meals together, and there was more intimacy in their union. They fell in love all over again.

At work, Eleanor felt a lot more engaged and fulfilled. As the shame of having something to hide was no longer the invisible wall blocking her light, she was now able to show up more authentically. As a result, she was now able to connect and collaborate with her coworkers and engage in problem-solving with the management skillfully and productively. This created win-win solutions and more opportunities to express and leverage her vision and talents, which led to her feeling happier and contributing more inspired, beautiful work.

Several months after Eleanor quit drinking, they

brought the happy news that she was pregnant. She gave birth to a beautiful baby girl.

As Eleanor healed, it became clear to her that all of her fears and anxieties had nothing to do with reality. She had spent years being tortured by her unanswered questions, feeling guilty for the depth of her desire, and confounded by her want of something that she didn't know she'd be able to have.

Her path to healing was through reconnecting with herself and with her inner child who was in need of healing. The transformation was amazing. She was able to step out of her experience of isolation, and show up more authentically at work, in her family, and in her marriage.

The way her partner showed up for her, without judgment, with a lot of love, compassion, and patience, created a stable and safe space necessary for her healing. I want to emphasize here that we're all human: we all have trauma, we all get triggered, and our defenses protect us all in different ways.

There is a legend that describes how a king sought to protect his daughter from hurt: She was out playing barefoot and pricked her foot on a thorn, and the king, distraught over her pain, ordered that the entire kingdom be covered in leather. His wise advisor suggested it may be more efficient to cover the princess's feet with leather instead, and this is how shoes were created.

Keith, Eleanor, and I worked together to learn how the trauma defenses operated within them, how they triggered each other, and over time we created custom-made "shoes" for both of them. And when both of them felt safe, there was no longer a need for defenses. Instead, there was trust. That's how we created the safe environment necessary for healing and creating deeper intimacy.

The exact same dynamic operates within teams and organizations. To create the safe work environment necessary for everyone to show up in their best creativity, teamwork, and productivity, we learn about our own triggers, and pick up the tools and materials to custom make those shoes, so the entire team can play together instead of being stuck in individual invisible inner prisons, pulling out thorns and bandaging wounds.

OUR IMPRISONED MINDS

To keep us from jailbreaking, our mind creates stories that hold us back from reaching for our goals, dreams, and desires beyond the prison walls. These stories may show up as self-doubt and imposter syndrome. In my clients' words we see how deeply these stories affect us.

"I feel like I need to do more. I'm not enough."

"I'm constantly juggling all the balls, and I feel guilty for not spending more time with my husband and children."

"I have overwhelming feelings of rage and helplessness."

When we identify these feelings in our lives, we may attempt to work on our mindset with self-development workshops and meditation, but simply changing our mindset will not secure our jailbreak. Our defense systems are very sophisticated, and when the prison guards in our mind sound the alarm, the rest of the prison guards come rushing in.

Isolation and shame have a purpose. They are defense mechanisms that protect us from the pain of our unmet desires. As one of my clients once said in a moment of realization:

> *"Shame is a fucked-up security blanket. I tell myself the stories that soothe me because they're what I know, not because they're truly good for me."*

Our prison guards want to keep us safely in the realm of the known. And what is known, is the prison of internalized patriarchal oppression that's been keeping women from being able to get in touch with—let alone claim—our true desires for millennia.

INVESTING IN THE DEFENSE COMPLEX

Every day I talk to high-achieving, successful women who are exhausted, who keep going-going-going, and at the end of the day, have trouble stopping, resting, and truly restoring.

Amid such exhaustion, there is so little space left for joy.

When we take a look together under the hood, a woman can see how her energy is actually being spent, what's keeping her wheels spinning and her engine running hot, driving her to exhaustion. We always discover a vindictive inner critic that questions her every move. She over-analyzes, questions her decisions, gets mired in self-doubt. The inner critic spins stories that keep her in a constant negotiation dance with her mind. To move forward even a baby step, she has to plan this elaborate chess game with her mind to make sure her thoughts don't kill her motivation, her ideas, her forward momentum, or her actions, before she can get to the next place on the chessboard.

Marie Forleo described this insidious voice in an interview for my podcast. Marie is a very successful entrepreneur and philanthropist whose programs have served hundreds of thousands of people and whose content reaches millions. "My inner critic, she's from Jersey," Marie said. "She's really, really, really harsh. Vicious at times."[14]

In an interview with Gayle King, Diane von Furstenberg said, "Most mornings I wake up and I feel like a

14   Marie Forleo, interviewed by Valerie Rein, "Use Your Gifts to Make Money, Change the World," *Her Success Radio*, February 6, 2018. Listen to the podcast at www.drvalerie.com/hersuccessradio.

loser." To which Gayle replied, "Most mornings I wake up and I feel fat."[15]

This dance of the mind is really the internalized oppression that patriarchy has inflicted upon women, by convincing us we are worth *less*. It puts us on a track to earn our worth by achievement. *If only I could lose fifteen pounds, if only I could find a good partner, if only I could be a better mother, I would be worthy.*

These thoughts are our prison guards. They execute the old instructions we received about how to survive in patriarchy by making sure we don't claim success on our own terms—and if we do—that we don't fully enjoy it. Not unlike the way our government spends more on defense than education, our biology dictates that we prioritize safety over thriving. As long as to our subconscious it feels unsafe to be visible, powerful, successful, happy, brilliant, and authentic, our prison guards will tell us stories to keep us safe inside our defined roles and identities issued by Patriarchy Press.

I estimate that around 90 percent of our energy is invested in maintaining the prison security system that includes the prison guards in our minds, bodies, and actions (MBA, for short). Check in with yourself: how much time daily do you spend battling self-sabotaging thoughts, distractions, losing your energy to addictions and attempts to undo their damage, or fighting the uphill battle of trying to get your motivation or your body, mood,

---

15 "Fashion Icon DVF on Success, Family and New Memoir," *CBS News,* November 10, 2014.

and energy to get on board with what you're up to? When I tell my clients this 90 percent estimation, the response I commonly get is, "At least."

Just imagine what you would be able to do if you reclaimed even 10 percent of the energy unconsciously invested in the prison security system—that would double your available resource! What would you want to consciously invest it in? Spending time with friends and loved ones, going for a walk or to see a movie, taking up painting, or learning how to make that chocolate soufflé? Before we can liberate our energy from the defenses, let's take a closer look at how they're serving us.

TRAUMA CREATES MISTRUST

We learn through experience. We touch a hot stove, we get burned, and we learn quickly not to touch it again. We share an opinion, it gets dismissed, and we learn that it is unsafe to speak our minds. We show up in the world looking beautiful and feeling happy, and we receive unwanted sexual attention. We learn it's unsafe to be beautiful. It's unsafe to be happy and careless. Over time, we learn to veil our beauty, our happiness, our brilliance in layers of defenses to keep us protected. We're careful not to touch the hot stove again.

With each of these experiences, we trust the world less. We trust ourselves less because we keep failing ourselves by doing things that get shut down, ridiculed, or transgressed upon. Violations of our boundaries—whether they are verbal, emotional, physical, or sexual—create a heartbreaking mistrust. We mistrust men. We mistrust other women. We police each other and ourselves. We mistrust our bodies, our judgment, and our inner knowing.

Many of my clients express that they don't relate to their body as their friend. They experience their body as something that has betrayed them—through a medical condition, unwanted physical or sexual experience, or simply by "not cooperating" with their goal weight. Most women are constantly at war with our bodies. It's not our fault. It's the millennia of the war on women and our bodies, internalized.

Intuition, our inner knowing, is another casualty of this war. According to patriarchy, logic trumps intuition. So we learned to devalue and mistrust our intuition. It is so easy, however, for the mind to manipulate logic and evidence. When trying to make a "rational" forward-thinking decision, consider this: the mind has no data about the future.

We do not know who we will be in the future, or what our capacity for dealing with triggers will be. Still, the mind takes the data about the past, filters it through the lens of trauma, and leads us to make choices about the future that are not always in our best interest. Such as, going for a "safe" job or a "safe" relationship, instead of that big opportunity or a relationship that you truly desire.

The mind says: *You can't have it. It's not for someone like you. It's too big, what if you fail?* When we operate at the level of logic, we're at the mercy of all our defenses. The prison guards call a meeting and convince us not to do anything that may threaten our safety. They know exactly how to hit us where it hurts, and exactly what to say to make us back down.

Recognizing these thoughts as prison guards that rationalize and wrap in stories the safety-seeking signals from our subconscious mind—which, neuroscientists tell us, *is* the actual decision-making authority—is one of the first steps on the jailbreak journey; it helps you reclaim the clarity and confidence in your decision-making.

Whenever I have let my "rational" thinking override my inner knowing, I have regretted that decision. While decisions I make intuitively—even if "illogical"—open possibilities for me beyond what I could have imagined or planned. Interestingly, many successful male founders and executives say that they rely on their intuition when making important decisions. Yet for many women this ability is compromised through the millennia of being punished and persecuted and ridiculed for using the power of our inner knowing. We need to realize that this mistrust of ourselves and what we know is internalized patriarchy, is a symptom of PSD, and heal it, so we can make decisions that are actually good for us and lead us to our desires—not away from them.

PRISON MOVIE NIGHT

To stop our jailbreak attempt, the prison guards interrupt our forward momentum by locking us in detention and putting on a movie that replays our old trauma. They want to make sure we never forget how unsafe it is out there. Our relationship with our prison guards functions in the same way an abusive relationship does to control us, by reminding us again and again how flawed we are, and how much safer it is here on the inside if we're careful and do all the right things. The punchline of the prison movie is always the same.

You don't know how good you have it with me. I love you so much, and there's no one out there who will love you as much as I do, with all your flaws and shortcomings. I mean, look at you.

Everything in the prison environment is built to confirm the story. Every action or inaction we take is designed to revolve around these defenses.

If we do all the right things and check off enough boxes, the guards tell us, we can have our privileges restored. More yard time. A cruise to Tahiti. The prison guards use these pleasurable experiences as rewards rather than choices we are "allowed" to make at any time.

You will know the prison guards by the way they make everything conditional.

The prison guards have favorite go-to stories they tell to manipulate our thinking and our choices. These stories pull our worth into question.

Who do you think you are?

Why would anyone want to listen to you?

Look at these wrinkles.

My breasts have the wrong shape.

Look at this flab, this cellulite, this sag, this puffiness.

The mind is a prolific author and a creative storyteller. It will weave a specific and descriptive tale, using the flavors of all the wounds and unhealed trauma, to ensure we never touch that trauma again. The prison guards call into question everything we do, and tell the stories that are most likely to undermine our confidence.

This overthinking stops us dead in our tracks. Particularly in relationships, these stories replay old traumas in our interpretations of our partner's behavior.

My husband doesn't pick up when I call him because he doesn't care about me.

He cares more about work than he cares about me. I'm invisible to him.

We're hijacked by trains of thought that leave the station so quickly, before you know it—*choo choo*—you're back in a memory of that one time you were in Chicago with that cheating boyfriend and it's freezing cold and you feel so betrayed and so alone. The trauma time machine makes an instant translation of that experience into present time—you feel alienated from your husband, you don't trust him and don't want to have sex with him.

Whatever the theme of our trauma, be it abandonment or betrayal or feeling unlovable, we're going to recreate these stories in our relationships again and again and again.

These traumas subconsciously guide our choices. If our trauma comes from a sense of being worth *less*, we're going to make sure we have a partner who thinks we're worth *less* and treats us that way. Perhaps he will say the right things and give us flowers and gifts, but he doesn't show up in the ways we truly need to support our visions and dreams. He doesn't step up to take care of the laundry when we need to be at that important meeting. He doesn't offer to take care of the kids when we need to go away on retreat and take care of ourselves. He behaves in ways our prison guards want him to do. He's a part of our internal reality, personified.

Our defenses show up in the stories we form about our experiences, and the choices we make that replay our trauma. Our prison guards protect from whatever makes sense to them to protect us from: embarrassment, heartbreak, abandonment, rejection.

The prison guards make everything conditional. We are only beautiful if we are the "right" size and shape. We are only worthy of love if we do and say the right things. We can only be successful if we work endlessly and achieve particular goals.

These are not our authentic stories. These are the stories of PSD. They may seem believable because they have been consistently with us our entire lives, but this does not make them true.

When the prison guards load up your old home movies, your old stories, begin to look for the conditional messages in them.

DRIVEN TO DISTRACTION

When we make efforts toward jailbreak, our prison guards come forward with the next level of defense: rationalization, procrastination, and distraction.

Let's say you begin a program to lose weight, and you start an exercise routine and make efforts to eat healthy. The mind quickly creates a rationalization to resist these changes. *I'll just skip one day. Nothing bad will happen if it's just one day.*

You may change your habits, but the prison guards know it is still dangerous to be beautiful in the world. This is what creates for many of us a sheath of invisibility in the way we dress, or the way we carry extra weight that is not healthy for us. We may change individual behaviors around the clothes we wear or our attempts to lose weight, but each threat of jailbreak will be met with an immediate response from the prison guards.

Weight loss is a loaded topic. The marketing of the majority of the industry is built on exploiting women's compliance with the patriarchal beauty standard. So there's that. Inherently, weight doesn't have anything to do with beauty—just like other beauty standards artificially imposed by patriarchy to control and manipulate women. Billions of dollars are poured into the beauty industry from the pockets of women desperate for more conditional love and acceptance.

We see this in all areas of our lives, including our work. Have you ever had the experience of working on an important project—one that will increase your visibility, advance your career, or bring new clients to your business—and the moment you even think about opening the document, you suddenly remember that you have to make a pediatrician's appointment for your son? Or take your car in for an oil change? Or a thousand other distractions pull you from the important work at hand?

Distractions are insidious because they're supported by the defenses on the level of the mind and the body. The mind rationalizes them: *this will only take a moment, and it's so important.* The body meanwhile senses that we're taking ourselves somewhere new, and it feels unsafe. It responds by clenching our jaws, shoulders, or guts. By breathing in a shallow pattern. By energy levels dropping, the mind speeding up.

Distraction has a very strong reinforcement loop, because it provides us with an immediate tension release. The moment you call the pediatrician or decide to take your car in instead of working on that document, you exhale. You feel lighter.

Similarly, countless women entrepreneurs have described working on a big project or a high-stakes deal and running into stumbling blocks to their success. They describe how they're stymied by an overwhelming mental fog or a lack of clarity and focus that hits as they try to work on the project. They wonder if they have adult ADD, and some already have that diagnosis.

When we look at ADD/ADHD through the lens of trauma, not only does it make sense as an effective trauma adaptation—as long as we remain distracted, we're not in our full power, and thus remain safe—a healing solution becomes clear. I've seen this with my clients over the years again and again. As we work on healing the underlying traumas, the symptoms of ADD resolve.

Ditto for anxiety and depression—which origins can also be traced to the trauma adaptations of fight or flight (anxiety) and freeze (depression) that over time with a lot of use become persistent states that severely interfere with our lives. Mind-body trauma resolution work has been the magic bullet that resolved my own anxiety and depression, as well as "adult ADD" before I knew it was a "thing," as well as so many of my clients'.

Viewing these conditions through the lens of trauma adaptations helps us see that they are not something that's "wrong with us"—they're actually appropriate reactions to trauma that have overstayed their welcome.

In the context of PSD, it's natural and adaptive to react to oppression with depression, and with anxiety to feeling unsafe. It's not "in our heads." It's been unsafe to be a woman for millennia. But just like women were termed "the weaker sex" after being suffocated in corsets led to anxiety, panic, and fainting caused by shallow breathing, women's natural reactions to the trauma of oppression are currently being pathologized and medicated.

In my fifteen years as a therapist, I rarely saw a high-achieving woman who was not medicated for anxiety, depression, sleep issues, ADD/ADHD and/or self-medicating with food, alcohol, work, or compulsive exercise. It's not women's fault—we all need to cope with pain to function. But when we take a big picture view of the origins of this pain that takes into account the ancestral, collective, and personal trauma, we can see that there's actually nothing wrong with us, and a healing solution beyond symptom management with medication emerges.

That's why I'm passionate about educating people about their mental health and sharing tools to take care of it outside of the therapy office. Just like we have the tools to take care of our physical health through paying attention to our bodies, what we eat, and what physical activity and rest we get. I hope that the insights and the tools that I share with you in this book empower you to take charge of your mental health and thrive, while forever exonerating you from the patriarchal charges that something is wrong with you and you need to be "fixed."

If distractions are propelled by the fight-or-flight reaction, another flavor of the prison guards in the action domain has to do with the freeze reaction. When you find yourself paralyzed in inaction, this is likely what you're experiencing. A client of mine, a successful businesswoman and a busy mom, was overwhelmed with handling the bulk of the housework, taking care of the kids, and trying to squeeze in self-care. Now and then, she would consider hiring some help—they could certainly afford it. But week after week, she would not take any steps toward making it happen. Each morning, she would just jump right back into the hamster wheel of managing it all and run even faster.

Deep down inside her subconscious, she did not feel she was worthy or entitled to this help. She came from a long line of hardworking women who always took care of their families, who always prepped all meals, and who always did everything that a good wife and a good mother was "supposed" to do. She had formed a subconscious commitment to what it meant to be a good wife and a good mother.

There's also another aspect to high-achieving women's addiction to staying busy and stressed. The adrenaline rush is empowering. Our body chemistry sends the signal to the subconscious—I'm fully charged, ready to outrun or fend off the danger! The chronic state of stress becomes an addiction, because like any other addiction it serves a function. It helps us disconnect and not feel challenging emotions, and it creates an illusion of empowerment and keeping us safe. Like any addiction, it has its unfortunate consequences. Adrenal fatigue and burnout have become an epidemic among high-achieving women. Behind it is a lethal combination of our internal engines running hot as a trauma adaptation and our productivity-oriented culture that equates achieving with worth and is pushing us to keep driving faster. Remember: They used to burn us at the stake. Now they just hand us the torches.

My client had a myriad of perfectly rational explanations for why she wasn't taking steps to hire help, and why she just had to say "yes" to every opportunity to get even busier and run even faster. If we look at the surface level of the situation, it just looks frustrating. Why don't you just hire help? Why don't you just say "no" to some things, so you can slow down and breathe? But now that we understand about how the invisible inner prison of PSD operates, we can clearly recognize these perfectly rational explanations as prison guards.

The prison guards were keeping her safe from slowing down and experiencing her own vulnerability. Dealing with issues in her marriage that she didn't want to face. Insecurities, self-doubt, and a vicious inner critic were there, at the door, waiting for her to open any amount of space to feel or think that they would immediately crowd in. So she didn't. She kept the door barricaded by busyness.

Consciously, she realized the situation was not sustainable and she was driving herself into exhaustion. That her irritability and fits of rage fueled by her nervous system being constantly in overdrive were causing arguments and alienation from her husband and children. Consciously, she really wanted to hire help and have a more sane and spacious schedule and life. But her subconscious had a different agenda—to keep her safe by keeping her busy. And the subconscious was winning, as it always does.

Does this story sound familiar? How are your prison guards keeping you safe? What are they helping you avoid? What would you experience if you didn't avoid it? Questions like these become a trail that will take you to the trauma that is asking to be healed.

OUR IMPRISONED BODIES

Women's relationships with our bodies have been severely traumatized by patriarchy. As a result, most of us don't experience our bodies as our friends—rather, they are things we have to manage and torture into compliance. We scheme about how we can squeeze more energy out of them or squeeze them into smaller-sized dresses with Spanx underneath. There's a disconnection in our relationship with our bodies, and it's not our fault.

We've internalized the trauma of the patriarchal war on our bodies.

Our modern-day corsets have evolved into board meetings, endless work hours, and household chores—just like the vintage shapeware, these don't let us catch our breath.

For millennia, women were not allowed to take up space and have autonomy and ownership anywhere, including in our own bodies. Women's bodies have always been controlled by patriarchal religions, social norms, and laws. Women's bodies used to be—and remain in some places of the world—men's property. We couldn't marry for love. We couldn't have sex when and with whom we desired. No wonder that many women struggle with accessing their sexual desire and have trouble with arousal and orgasms: the desire is controlled by prison guards, because it is dangerous.

There's nothing more dangerous to patriarchy than a woman who's in touch with her desire. Sexual desire is as integral to who we are as human beings as breathing. It's an inalienable part of human, authentic expression. It's the beating heart that pumps the juice of every other desire. Dial it down, and you'll dial down a woman's life force, drive, and shine in every area of her life.

Prison guards also regulate our sex lives through internalized patriarchal judgments that police women's bodies. Talking about how PSD affects her, one woman described her experience of sex this way: "Every time I'm naked in bed with my partner, I feel like there are twenty people in the room—watching, judging."

Another area of women's relationship with our bodies that has been devastated by patriarchal oppression is our menstrual cycle. The distorted messages we've received growing up about our cycle range from not talking about menstruation at all with our own mothers, to having experiences that shame us and make us feel our bodies are somehow wrong.

This sense of wrongness carries into adulthood. Because we operate in a linear masculine paradigm, as a culture, we don't honor the natural cyclical ebb and flow of creativity. We repress our natural cycles so in order to keep producing consistently each day.

Then our bodies revolt with challenging symptoms associated with premenstrual syndrome, premenstrual dysphoric disorder, perimenopause, and menopause. This is the body's way of saying, *How long can you oppress me? I'm speaking to you. Hear me, tend to me.*

What do we do in response to that voice? We take medication. To fix our adrenals and thyroids, to sleep, to focus, to stop the panic, to keep from crying...Patriarchy supplies a pill for every symptom of PSD.

OVERRIDING OUR BIOLOGY

Recently I saw a post on social media asking for help. "I'm working on this important project," the woman had written. "I'm struggling with energy and focus. What can I do?"

There were several hundred comments, all offering hacks of some kind for how to increase energy. They suggested herbs, supplements, and coached her on strategies to push through her fatigue.

None of the comments said, "well, maybe you need to rest?" In the patriarchal culture, where our worth is attached to our output, the pressure—both external and internalized—is to keep the foot on the gas pedal. Rest—the state of the feminine creative—is devalued as all things that have to do with feminine power.

There's another aspect to women's struggle with energy and focus that has to do with prison guards that are keeping them safe from stepping into their power.

From my work with women entrepreneurs, I knew this might be the key. This woman was stepping into the next level of her visibility, her bigness. What were the stakes? Remember how much energy we invest into the defense complex. It follows that we would naturally experience energy depletion when we are stretching ourselves; this is when deep parts of ourselves can feel unsafe and the prison guards are working overtime, usurping so much more of our energy.

My advice to this woman would have been: "Don't try to override and overpower them. Tend to them and hear what they have to say."

This is counter to the advice we see plastered across social media, such as "Punch fear in the face!" "Fear is a lie!" "The only thing stopping you is you!" This advice that we often hear from self-help gurus follows the patriarchal model of achievement by oppression, suppression, and domination. This advice has to do with overriding our biology and denying, neglecting, and abusing those parts of ourselves that have already been denied, neglected, and abused.

Not only is it not effective, it has terrible consequences for our mental health. Clients came to me after they developed panic attacks using affirmations with words in them that were triggering their trauma. Such as, repeating an affirmation with the word "safe" when our body, our biology feels unsafe, making the biological fear response rev up more to get our attention. What started at a little bit of anxiety can escalate into a full-blown panic attack.

Another danger of these "power through" and "break through" approaches that attempt to override our biology is that they are not effective—and women are wired to see failures as our fault. As a woman keeps running in the self-help hamster wheel, these "failures" keep accumulating as "evidence": *since nothing that the gurus teach is working for me, I must be broken beyond repair, something is terribly wrong with me.*

Recently, ads from this very successful world-renowned coach have been flashing across my social media feed, that say, in all caps, *DOMINATE YOUR COMPETITION*. Check in with yourself, how does your body respond to reading this? And your mind?

This violent blueprint of external success has been intrinsic to the patriarchal ethos. We've internalized this ethic of domination and oppression. We try to dominate ourselves into submission and compliance. We push ourselves into doing, doing, doing, until our body screams, *Don't do this! I am tired. Stop doing this to me.*

When we try to override these defenses of the body by changing our mindset and pushing through anyway, the body's defenses double down. As a result, we have all these high-achieving women whose bodies have been paying the patriarchal toll on their success.

I ended up in the ER. Many of my clients have experienced adrenal fatigue, issues with sleep, digestion, and weight, hormonal imbalances, and autoimmune disease. The mind-body connection of these conditions is well established. I believe that uncovering the hidden traumas and understanding how they play out in the mind-body relationship can be the missing piece in the holistic healing picture.

THE NERVOUS SYSTEM IN ACTION

The human autonomic nervous system has two divisions—sympathetic and parasympathetic; it controls internal body processes and operates largely unconsciously. The prison guards are the agents of the sympathetic nervous system. This is the system that activates the fight-or-flight stress response. Inside the PSD prison, the sympathetic system is on most of the time. The prison guards are constantly on alert for anything that might make us feel exposed and unsafe.

THE SYMPATHETIC NERVOUS SYSTEM

When our sympathetic nervous system is activated, it slows down the processes that restore, rejuvenate, and rebuild the body. This includes sleep, digestion, and cell repair. These functions aren't our primary concern when we're in survival mode; instead, all of our resources go toward our safety.

Constant stress ages us. Staying in this state for periods of time creates wear and tear on the body. Because sympathetic activation interferes with our digestion, we don't absorb nutrients optimally or eliminate toxins effectively. Stress-related health conditions are tied back to time spent in this state. Luckily, the parasympathetic system balances and repairs the damage done.

THE PARASYMPATHETIC NERVOUS SYSTEM

When the parasympathetic nervous system is activated, our heart rate slows, the relaxation response kicks in, and activity in our glands and intestines increases. With the body established in safety and relaxation, it can begin cell reproduction and rejuvenation activities, including digestion.

It's through establishing embodied safety and relaxation that we can help repair the body and the mind. There are simple techniques, based in ancient practices, such as yoga, that can help shift the level of nervous system activation within minutes. You can learn more about and experience some of these practices on my website.

JOURNALING
TRACKING THE PRISON GUARDS

We've now seen the various ways that the prison guards show up in the domains of the mind, body, and action. Remember that the prison guards are trying to keep you safe; they're not bad guys. We jailbreak not by trying to push through them or get rid of them; instead, we start by meeting, greeting, acknowledging and thanking them for working around the clock to keep us safe.

As you go through your day, notice any moments when you feel blocked from your fullest expression. When you're trying to do or say something, and instead you stop in your tracks, what's getting in your way? Keep a log of your observations.

- Write down the triggering event. What was the moment that stopped you?
- In that moment, how did the prison guards show up in the mind? What thoughts or stories did they tell?
- Notice what that block felt like in your body. Did it show up

as a craving for something sweet, anxiety, or depressed energy?

- What prison guards showed up in your actions? Write down any distractions or addictive behaviors you noticed.

I encourage you to notice in the moment when these guards show up and capture your observations in a log over the course of your day. If you cannot write them down in the moment, make a mental note and take time at the end of the day to add to your log. You can download the log form from my website www.drvalerie.com.

Through this exercise, you'll gain a greater understanding of the workings of the prison security system and what's really stopping you. Here's the key: *You are not stopping yourself. You are not getting in your own way.* Prison guards are parts of the defense system, and once you get to know them, you can train them to become your bodyguards in the next step of jailbreak.

ANSWERING THE CALL

Through the stories they spin, the distractions they create, and the symptoms they express through the body, our prison guards work tirelessly to keep us from touching our trauma. As a result, we stay up in our heads, out of our bodies—when the body carries unprocessed trauma, the head is the only safe place to be. Maintaining the prison security system takes massive amounts of our energy.

The solution is not to override, but to listen. When we truly allow ourselves to feel our body's needs and requests, we begin to see our clues for healing.

Along this jailbreak journey, every new awareness is a huge win, whether you decide to do anything about it yet. You'll begin to ask different questions.

What would you do if you had all this energy back? How would you reinvest it? Where would you consciously invest your energy if you no longer had to maintain this defense complex?

My call to you is to *celebrate* every time you encounter a prison guard. Every word of the inner critic, every distraction, and every inconvenient sensation from your body. Use it as an opportunity to get curious about what this particular defender is protecting you from. Getting angry, pouring another drink, eating a pint of ice cream on your seventh episode of a streaming show binge—what happens when you begin to see these not as character flaws, but as safety mechanisms protecting you from pain?

What becomes possible when you show up authentically in your life, work, and relationships, vulnerable and empowered, present and open, defense-less? You reclaim so much energy. Can you feel it from just reading these words? You can lose weight without trying because your body is no longer on cortisol overload, making you overeat for safety and magically storing twice the amount you eat as fat. Your financial health can improve because you're no longer shopping to numb disquieting feelings or shying away from opportunities to play—and get paid—big. You can transform your experience when facing a challenge. Fear and excitement are the same rush of energy. Fear is that energy blocked by the prison guards who say, *you can't do that*. Excitement is that energy liberated.

When we recognize our defenses—in our mental filters, thoughts and stories, distractions and self-sabotage, and our body's signals—we can follow the clues they leave behind.

As we get to know our prison guards, we discover what they're protecting us from and learn to collaborate with them as we proceed on our jailbreak journey.

CHAPTER THREE

BRIBING THE GUARDS

The longest journey is from the head to the heart.

—ANONYMOUS

YOUR PRISON GUARDS JUMP INTO ACTION WHEN-ever they feel there's a threat to your safety—being safely imprisoned, that is. When we can create that safety in our being, when our whole system feels safe—the guards can go back to playing cards.

When the prison guards are on break, we are no longer fighting the toxic thoughts, the tension in our bodies, the procrastination, the resistance, or any number of other techniques the prison guards use to keep us in line.

We get that energy back.

When the guards are on break, we can make our jailbreak. We can enjoy life and create our magic in the world.

Think back to the last time you left your house to go somewhere.

What did the light look like outside?

How did the temperature feel?

What scents were in the air?

Do you remember much about how you ended up at the grocery store, or at work, or back home?

We so often move through our lives on autopilot, and we miss so much of our surroundings. This is a symptom of spending our lives up in our heads, chatting with our prison guards, away from our bodies. And this way of living is robbing us of the full experience of life.

In this chapter, I share with you some exercises that are designed to bring us back into our bodies and help create embodied safety.

MIND-BODY: DIVIDE AND CONQUER

One of the core patriarchal wounds stems from separating the mind from the body and establishing the mind as superior to the body. In this system, the body—with all its wisdom, intuition, and sexual power—has been denigrated, disregarded, and demonized. We were trained to listen to logic over our own intuitive knowing.

The flaw in the system is that the mind operates with a very limited data set. It doesn't have any data about the future. The information it gleans from the past and present is filtered through the matrix of trauma-shaped perception. This process takes much of our energy, as each of the prison guards analyzes this data against the specific trauma they've been charged with protecting us from.

We get stuck in the mind because of the energetics of trauma. Trauma is an embodied experience of feeling unsafe, and it creates defensive contraction.

Imagine that this energy, the energy of our emotions, runs through channels in the body. When we feel unsafe, the channels contract. The emotional expression gets interrupted. Trauma leaves a trail of unprocessed, "stuck" emotional energy in the body.

Over time, the body becomes a minefield of frozen emotions and we learn to stay out of there and hang out in our heads instead. It doesn't feel safe to go down into the body.

It's a vicious cycle: we stay in our heads, and this feeds overanalyzing, worry, and anxiety. In order to discharge the energy of trauma that's frozen in the body, we need to get into the body and move it out.

MANAGING MICROAGGRESSIONS

Our lives are full of microtriggers that activate traumas all day long: situations and exchanges that make us feel subconsciously unsafe and trigger PSD and other traumas. Whenever we feel dismissed, disregarded, our boundaries violated, or that our contribution is devalued, our escape from the body and into the head—as well as other trauma reactions—may get triggered.

Psychiatrist Chester M. Pierce coined the term *micro-aggressions* in the 1970s to describe insults and dismissals African Americans regularly experienced. Psychologists since broadened the understanding of this phenomenon to apply to any socially marginalized group, based on race, gender, sexual orientation, social class, and ability status. Psychologist Derald Wing Sue, who was my professor in at Teachers College, Columbia University, defines micro-aggressions as "brief, everyday exchanges that send denigrating messages to certain individuals because of their group membership."[16] The person, group, organization, or the entire culture sending these messages does so unconsciously and is unaware of their effect.

Microaggressions are insidious and their effects are toxic. For example, Stanford University psychology professor Claude Steele has found that priming African Americans and women with racial and gender stereotypes negatively affected their academic performance.[17]

My client Stacey recently left her male-dominated firm, where she experienced microaggressions daily for twenty years. For most of these years, she was not conscious of them, because in order to survive and build a successful career in a traditionally male industry, she had subconsciously abandoned her identity as a woman at work and operated like a man.

---

16   Paludi, M. A., *Managing Diversity in Today's Workplace.* Praeger Publishing, 2012.

17   Tori DeAngelis, "Unmasking 'Racial Micro Aggressions,'" *American Psychological Association,* 2009, 40(2): 42.

It was only after she "made it" to the top leadership tier of the firm that sexism became an inescapable reality. She found herself the only woman at the table, and the only person whose contributions were consistently dismissed, and whose input was devalued. There was no room to hide in denial of her membership in the woman tribe anymore; she'd become as much like a man as she could, and yet she was still being subjected to microaggressions like a woman.

She cut off the traditionally feminine traits such as emphasizing emotions and interpersonal connections, and this had resulted in managerial struggles. She didn't engage fully with people, she missed the emotional context of communication between the lines, and she saw a rise in employee conflict and poor performance. At home she operated similarly, in a chief executive capacity. Her relationships with her husband and children stayed at surface level. The children were just doing their own thing. Stacey's sex life was nonexistent.

This was not her fault or her failure or a shortcoming. Subconsciously, she knew there was no room for her wholeness in the organization where she worked, and as a result, she stayed squarely in the head and in her logical mind. She experienced casualties as a result of this survival strategy. Her relationships at work and at home began to suffer, and her mental health suffered as well—she was on medication for depression and anxiety.

Stacey went through a deep crisis as she realized the

toll that denying her womanhood had taken on her happiness, well-being, and her relationship with her family. She then embarked on her journey of reclamation of her authentic self. Much of this work has taken her into learning to inhabit her body again, after decades spent almost exclusively in her head.

Stacey is not alone. Many of my clients and other accomplished women I know came to this same realization—that they had been able to fly under the radar of PSD by subconsciously separating themselves from everything the society told them they were, could, and could not do, as women. But with that, they also abandoned a lot of what was authentic to them as human beings. This is how trauma operates—when we defensively shut off the part of the experience that feels dangerous and unwanted, we also lose access to other parts.

The price that they paid for it included chronic illness; divorce or alienation from their spouse; an unsatisfying, challenging, or non-existent sex life; distant relationships with their children; years on prescription medications for anxiety and depression; drinking more than socially; eating more than they know is optimal for their health; impulsive decisions made from the head, without participation from their intuition. PSD and other traumas and their adaptations had blocked these women's inner knowing—including knowing themselves. Again and again, I would hear them say, "I just want to feel like myself again." When we would unpack it further, this meant to them feeling authentic, embodied, whole, and fully alive versus like a dead woman walking.

Women as well as people of color, LGBTQ+, people with disabilities, and other marginalized groups, deal with microaggressions all day long. Traumas being constantly triggered cause people chronic stress and dangerous disconnection from our bodies, our full authentic lives, our authentic way of being and relationships. Our society pays a price: the greatest gifts that women and members of socially marginalized groups bring are not being realized.

Frequent microaggressions in the workplace repress creativity and productivity, increase absenteeism and presenteeism (when a person is physically present but mentally checked out), and drive diverse talent out the door. Sadly, many companies are unaware of how their cultures support microaggressions. But we're living at the time when customers and businesses are becoming more attuned and discerning, and the costs of ignoring the issue are staggering. At a recent shareholder meeting of a company with a heavily male-dominated leadership team and culture, a shareholder brought up a concern that their top talent—all diverse individuals—was leaving, because the company culture was hostile to them. The leadership team was stumped. They surely did not set out to create a culture that would be hostile to anyone. They were not aware that their company culture was toxic for diverse talent, let alone what was creating this environment.

Just like individuals, companies, communities, and cultures too, have unprocessed traumas that need healing. The healing journey begins with awareness—that is often challenging and painful, but it opens the door to forging a new, conscious path of being, where a safe environment can be created for all to feel valued with their diverse and wonderful talents and contributions, and thrive in their authentic expression.

EXERCISE: YOUR RE-POWER TOOL

Your power is in your presence. Your embodied presence.

Many times throughout the day, traumas gets triggered, you feel subconsciously unsafe, and move out of the body and into the head. This exercise is designed to support you in re-inhabiting your body by sending a message to your hindbrain, that at this particular moment, nothing is threatening your actual physical safety. As we discussed before, the hindbrain doesn't speak the language of words, notions, and logic. There's nothing you can *say* to effectively shift your state out of the fight-or-flight response. It speaks the language of experience. This exercise is designed to help you communicate to your hindbrain in the language that it understands, the language of the senses, and send the message that it's safe to come back into the body—in three minutes or less, by connecting with your awareness of the following:

1. **GRAVITY.** Take a moment to feel your feet on the floor. Feel the sensations in your feet, and the pull of gravity that connects you to the ground. Feel the sensations of your body in contact with the furniture. Feel the secure embrace of the earth, physically holding and supporting you.

2. **BREATH.** Feel the breath moving through your body. Feel how supported you are by your breath. No matter what's going on around you, your breath is reliably happening. Just like gravity, it's always there for you.

3. **FIVE SENSES.** Touch something in your environment. Take in the environment through your gaze. Listen to the sounds around you. Open up to receiving information about the environment through the senses of smell and taste.

Notice the difference in your energy before you began the exercise, and after. Now that you have experienced the baseline of embodiment, see if you can notice throughout the day, when you get pulled out of your body and into your head and use this practice to come back into the power of your embodied presence.

If you'd like me to guide you through this practice, download an audio recording of the Re-Power Tool at www.drvalerie.com.

IDENTIFYING DISEMBODIMENT

In an average day we encounter countless triggers that remind us it's not safe to be in our bodies, and we end up hanging out up in our heads.

We can see this in the way we eat. Eating a beautiful meal can be a fully embodied experience. When we fully enjoy a meal, we feel satiated, satisfied, and nourished. By contrast, emotional eating can be a disembodied experience that we use to numb some emotion that we don't want to feel.

Take it a step further: consider your sex life.

Your sexual experiences—and how satisfying they are, or not—have a lot to say about whether it feels safe for your energy to be in your body. How accessible is sexual pleasure to you? How easily do you get aroused? How easily do you orgasm?

These questions can be frustrating because we're conditioned to feel shame and guilt around our sexual expression. If you experience lack of pleasure in your sexual experiences, it's not your fault. This is the same mechanism of trauma at play. Your defenders keep you safe by moving this energy out of your body and into your head.

And then when you're having sex, you're kind of there, but not fully there.

Remember the woman who shared that when she's having sex, it feels like there are twenty people watching and judging her? Can you relate to these tirades of the inner critic? *Look at your body. Look at these folds. Look at the cellulite. Do you look attractive? Do you look like you're enjoying it? Are you doing everything he wants you to? Is he enjoying this? He's going to cheat on you if he doesn't enjoy sex with you...*

This kind of PSD-induced pressure makes it very hard to be embodied in the experience.

It does not take a revolution of your lifestyle to have more pleasure in your life. You can do it now. Below you'll find another practice that is designed to further support your embodiment. After you use the Re-Power Tool to move out of your head—filled with judgmental voices— and into your body, use this practice to help your nervous system settle into safety and relaxation. When we feel safe and relaxed, pleasure becomes available.

By the way, relaxation does not automatically ensue from sitting on the couch and watching TV with a glass of wine and a bag of chips. Alcohol provides a shortcut to the parasympathetic nervous system by stimulating the release of γ-Aminobutyric acid, more commonly known as GABA—a neurotransmitter that has an inhibitory action on the nervous system and promotes relaxation. But within an hour or so, GABA levels fall again, and you need another glass of wine to keep it going. Anti-anxiety medications have a very similar mechanism of action.

Learning the tools and building the skills to shift from *stressed* to *safe* to *pleasure* at will and without substances is indeed revolutionary. Remember, there's nothing more dangerous to patriarchy than a woman who's in touch with her desire. When you begin to make space for pleasure in your daily life, your desire awakens, and begins directing your choices, big and small. From the choice of glass you use to drink water (does it give you pleasure?) to the socks you wear (do they give you pleasure?) to your work situation (does it give you pleasure?).

When you put pleasure on your radar, it begins to pull forth the best out of you, it begins to recalibrate your life, consciously shape it as designed by your authentic desires—for your true well-being, deeply nourishing relationships, and the fullest expressions of your talents in your work in the world. You're no longer at the mercy of the circumstances—you consciously align them to support your desires. You reclaim your sovereignty. You become unstoppable.

EXERCISE: THREE-PART BREATH

So often in the PSD prison, our nervous system runs in chronic hyperactivation. This exercise, that comes from yoga, is designed to help you bribe the guards. By paying deliberate attention to our breath, we can shift the nervous system from survival-oriented sympathetic activation to parasympathetic activation that sets in motion the mechanisms that support our thriving. This shift can happen in a very short amount of time, over just a few breaths. Regular practice of the following breathing exercise creates a cumulative effect: Your body remembers how to relax, it becomes easier and easier to access relaxation on demand, and over time your baseline of nervous system activation shifts, melting decades of chronic stress, and helping you make a relaxed state a new normal. Which also happens to be your more productive and creative state where you make clearer and better decisions.

This breath can be practiced sitting or lying down. Start in the position where you feel most comfortable.

Place one hand on your chest and the other hand on your belly.

Imagine that your whole torso is a vessel that you're going to fill with air. You'll pour the air in, like pouring liquid into a glass.

First, pour into the belly. Relax your abdomen to expand as a slow inhale moves into your lungs and pushes down on the diaphragm.

As you continue to inhale, allow the ribs to splay out, creating more space in the ribcage.

Inhale some more, and feel the air expand your back and chest. Feel your collarbones rise at the top of your inhale.

Begin to exhale from the top, allowing your collarbones and shoulders to descend.

Allow the muscles surrounding your ribs and chest to return to neutral.

Finally, allow your belly to return to neutral. At the bottom of your exhale, gently pull your belly in to complete the exhalation.

Repeat this inhale-exhale cycle for three or four rounds. If you feel dizzy or lightheaded, simply return your breath to normal.

Make your inhales and exhales approximately the same length. You can count as you take each breath in and then slowly release it. Over time, with practice, you may naturally feel that the exhalation wants to linger a little longer. If you're already feeling it, go with that, let your exhalations be longer than inhalations. Longer exhalations further promote the relaxation response.

After completing this breath, you may yawn or feel more tired, especially if you've been pushing yourself beyond your capacity. Your stomach may growl, and you may feel your digestion activating. These are all signs that your nervous system is shifting from the sympathetic to the parasympathetic activation, i.e., you're relaxing—without wine, food, or TV. Great job!

This three-part breath encourages your diaphragm to increase its range of motion. It helps the muscles that may be habitually carrying tension to experience relaxation. The belly has the opportunity to soften and expand, and because we often have shame that gets encoded into our relationship with our bellies, this exercise can also support us in healing PSD and other traumas underlying this shame by actively bringing love, kindness, and gentleness to the belly.

Pay attention to pleasurable sensations as you breathe, rather than worrying whether you're doing it "right." If you are paying attention to your body, no matter how many times your mind gets distracted, you're doing it right.

This is a lovely practice to do at the end of the day as you're preparing to go to sleep, but you can also do it throughout the day to take a break. If your nervous system tends to run hot—if you tend to find yourself stressed and anxious throughout the day or have a hard time falling asleep or staying asleep through the night—practice this breath frequently to tone the nervous system, to tap the breaks on the sympathetic activation regularly, so at the end of the day your engine can slow down with more ease. Set a timer for once an hour to take a few three-part breaths—for one to three minutes at a time—and watch your pleasure bank account grow, your productivity and creativity increase, your reactivity and impulsivity decrease, your relationships improve, your choices become better and more effortless—because when you're out of the trauma hijack, out of the head and in your body, you're actually in touch with your intuition.

The breath is the bridge between the body and the mind, between the subconscious and the conscious. If you check in with yourself throughout the day, your breath will tell you how you're feeling. Shallow breaths in the chest are a signal that your sympathetic nervous system is activated and running its fight-or-flight program. Bringing deep breaths into your belly and attending to the pleasurable sensations in your body can help your system make the switch to relaxation, where your system is actually available to experience pleasure.

Would you like to breathe together? I've recorded a video of this practice for you. You can watch it at—you guessed it!— www.drvalerie.com.

TRAINING YOUR ATTENTION TO PLEASURE

Treat paying attention to pleasure as a training curriculum. If you want to wake up and feel happy every morning, then practice it: Take ten seconds before you get out of bed to feel the pleasurable texture of your sheets, the temperature of your skin, the quality of the light, the sounds in the room. Move and stretch gently and take pleasure in the sensations of your body being able to move. If self-judgment pops up, bring your awareness back to the sensations—you can't be in your body and up in your head at the same time. The more you practice, the more your capacity to experience pleasure expands and your pleasure "bank account" grows.

You may be wondering, what's so important about pleasure? Why do I need to train myself to feel it? Great question. For women under patriarchy, there's always been a prohibition on pleasure. Any kind of pleasure—sexual, the pleasure and satisfaction in her work in the world, the pleasures of everyday life...A woman's existence was only justified by her utility as a dutiful wife and mother. Her life was in service to the pleasure of men—not her own. A woman's world was defined by patriarchal norms and expectations, and punishments for going against them were severe. No wonder that many women struggle with pleasure, from sexual arousal and orgasms to creating her life designed by her desires—not compromising who she loves or what she does for work, to how she dresses, looks, and talks, and the choices she makes around having children and parenting.

Reclaiming the full range of our pleasure is reclaiming our sovereignty, our right to color our lives outside the lines of their utility to patriarchy.

As you might expect, prison guards are protecting access to pleasure. At a jailbreakers' retreat, my client Patty described how each time she paid attention to her pleasure, she would also feel a constriction in her throat. This is not an uncommon response: it's the prison guards sounding the alarm that it's unsafe to take our attention down into the body. For Patty, this constriction was keeping her energy up in her head, in the analytical mind, which felt both familiar and safe.

Notice when your attention slips back into the mind, where you're at the mercy of the prison guards. Bring your attention back to the sensations of your body embraced by gravity, solidly supported by the floor and furniture. Bring your attention back to your breath. See if opening to pleasure is a possibility. When you do notice pleasure, focus on the sensory experience of it. Anchoring in the sensations of the body helps keep us from getting caught and circulated in the stories of the mind.

EXERCISE: INVITING TOUCH

Touch creates instant comfort for our nervous systems. It promotes oxytocin release. Oxytocin is a neurotransmitter that, among other things, supports bonding, relaxation, boosts sexual arousal, induces sleep, and relieves stress. It builds on the safety that we've created with the Re-Power Tool and the Three-Part Breath and takes us a step further, into relaxation and pleasure. What's more, experiencing sensory pleasure anchors us in the body versus the anxious mind.

Children instinctively use touch to create a sense of safety for themselves. They curl up in a ball, rock rhythmically back and forth, and use this contact with their bodies to self-soothe. Touch promotes a feeling of safety and pleasure.

Touch seduces us into deeper embodiment.

Return to the Re-Power Tool: Feel the sensations of your feet in contact with the floor. Feel the sensations of your body supported by the furniture. Feel the movement of your breath. Take in your environment through your five senses. Follow up with two to three rounds of the Three-Part Breath.

Now add self-soothing touch. Stroke your face and feel the sensations on your skin. Touch your own face like you would touch a child or a puppy—with tenderness and unconditional love. Massage your forehead, temples, and cheekbones. Stroke your arms, your hands, your legs, or whatever area of your body wants to invite touch. Let every touch affirm your preciousness. Experiment with the level of pressure until you dial it in to exactly what feels pleasurable to you. This practice can be done with a partner too, but I highly recommend practicing it solo on a regular basis.

SHIFT TO SAFETY

The more you encourage parasympathetic activation through the exercises in this chapter, the more you train your nervous system to change the baseline of where it habitually hangs out from sympathetic to parasympathetic activity.

These practices signal to the entire mind-body system that you are safe. In this way, you are supporting your physical health, your emotional health, and ultimately your jailbreak—your shift from surviving to thriving.

Our survival is rooted in the principle of safety first. Without safety, our prison guards will not allow us to fully access our trauma so it can be reprocessed, integrated, and we can begin to tunnel out. The guards exist for a reason. If it feels unsafe to go to those depths, the guards will block trauma even from our memories, let alone from our daily awareness. The body remembers everything, however, and for her to grant us access to healing, she needs to feel safe.

Establishing embodied safety is the first step to not only appease the prison guards, but also to resource ourselves and restore our energy for jailbreak. If we invest less energy in our defenses, we have more energy for the journey.

Relaxation signals to the prison guards that there's nothing to worry about. After all, we wouldn't be this relaxed if we weren't safe. Relaxation *is* the embodied experience of feeling safe. Most women in our culture have no reference point for it.

Remember the story I told in chapter 1, about my introduction to yoga? That day, when I finally got through the entire class and landed in *savasana*, I felt so deeply relaxed like I've never felt before. I knew what I was feeling was an entirely new experience for me. That day, for the first time in my life, I felt safe and secure in my body.

On the jailbreak journey, you learn to generate this experience of embodied safety at will. The prison guards go back to playing cards. And you can proceed with the jailbreak plans you've been hatching and pursue the desires you've been incubating.

CHAPTER FOUR

DIGGING THE TUNNEL

Of all the things trauma takes away from us, the worst is our willingness, or even our ability, to be vulnerable. There's a reclaiming that has to happen.

—BRENÉ BROWN, *RISING STRONG*

THE FIRST TIME LINDA CAME TO MY OFFICE, THERE was a palpable sense of stress packed into her body. She carried some extra weight, and she hunched her shoulders like she was trying to take up less space in the room. She was visibly uncomfortable. She sat at the edge of the really big chair, as if she didn't want to inconvenience it with her presence. As she spoke about her situation, her gestures and her speech were subdued. She was working hard to contain her body, her feelings, and emotions from taking up any space.

There was no space for her feelings and emotions at work. She was in a leadership position, and there was no place for that. There was no space to express herself at home because she was so careful to protect her husband from being concerned. Her girlfriends led very different lives from hers, and they couldn't relate to her issues. She didn't want to burden them.

I realized as she talked that she was giving voice to her feelings for the first time in a long time. Underneath the specific situation she was discussing were packed years of pain and stress. Food was her ally in keeping a lid on her emotions.

Linda had been betrayed at work. A subordinate that she'd been mentoring and supporting for years had suddenly turned against her and was creating chaos at the company. Linda didn't experience this as a betrayal at first; instead, she felt helpless in the face of this animosity, and she felt immense pressure to solve the issue. She didn't know how to handle the situation and all her feelings.

We began our work together by creating basic safety, through practices similar to the Re-Power Tool. I encouraged her to take up more space in her chair. The first time she slid back and allowed her body to take up space, she smiled sheepishly. As I prompted her to explore the comfort and pleasure of her body being fully supported by the chair, her smile grew mischievous. I began to see the real Linda peek through the contained façade. I just couldn't wait for more of the authentic her to come out, I was eager to get to know her.

As we deepened our work together, she discovered that she felt her body had betrayed her. Linda had a chronic medical condition that was very disruptive in her life, and her body felt like anything but her friend. She was angry at her body, both for betraying her with the medical condition, and with the extra weight, which she hated.

Linda befriended her body, little by little, and her body became her ally in healing. I taught her to create embodied safety and she began to appreciate her body for helping her have that experience. Little by little, she was able to take that embodied safety into the work situation. She was able to be more present in meetings, even when the meetings felt hostile and she wasn't well supported by her colleagues. This was a notable shift from how previous meetings had gone for her, when she experienced such a strong fight-or-flight reaction that she would freeze, unable to articulate her point of view. She now walked taller, smiled broader, and spoke up. She began to take up space in her life.

DIGGING DOWN TO THE GOLD

As we dove deeper, hidden trauma emerged that was being triggered by Linda's work situation. She had been sexually abused as a little girl. In this horrifying and shattering experience, she'd felt scared, hurt, helpless, and betrayed. The work situation triggered and stirred up this trauma. The trauma time machine made her feel now like she felt then as a little girl—scared, hurt, helpless, and betrayed. Just like it did then, her body went into freeze, and she was feeling paralyzed and unable to fight back.

Linda shared that it was the first time she'd spoken about her experience of abuse. She had been in therapy before for years, but she'd never shared it.

I don't claim to know why Linda chose this moment to share this experience for the first time, but my sense of it is that perhaps establishing safety in her body was a prerequisite that made it safe for her to touch her trauma and talk about it.

Before she could go there, she first needed to create a safe container that allowed her to be supported. With a strong enough container, she could revisit the experience without falling apart. She knew she would be okay, that she would survive.

Using the resources she'd accumulated in our work together thus far, I helped her connect to the little girl who had had a life-altering, deeply traumatic experience. Linda was able to bring those resources, along with her love, affection, understanding, and compassion, to the little girl.

Linda was able to acknowledge and validate the little girl's feelings, and she recognized that back then, as in her adult life, she hadn't felt there was room for her feelings and emotions. She never told anyone. She never told her parents. She didn't feel it would matter or make a difference. She was also protecting her parents from the pain of knowing that something bad had happened to her and blaming themselves. Instead, she took on all of the pain and blame and carried them in her body for decades.

As an adult woman in a leadership position, she had continued to carry her feelings and emotions inside. She had a strong façade, but inside she was hurting. The work situation triggered the feelings of intense fear, helplessness, and desperation that her body had imprinted at the time of her trauma.

Linda was finally able to create space for the feelings she'd experienced as a little girl. She was able to let her inner child know that her feelings mattered, that she was very sorry there had been no one to protect her, and that she was now there to take care of her.

THE RED DRESS

After she established a loving, trusting, and supportive connection with this young part of herself, amazing things began to happen in Linda's life. She reclaimed the playfulness, vitality, and joy that her five-year-old self had naturally embodied, but that had been locked away by trauma for so long—it hadn't felt safe to go there.

The little Linda had loved to dress up in fancy dresses and a variety of colors. The adult Linda reclaimed this playfulness. One day, she walked into my office, regally as she did now, slid all the way into the depth of the chair, leaned back comfortably, and gave me her signature mischievous smile. She shared, sparkly and giddy with excitement, that she had worn a red sleeveless dress to a party.

She felt like a queen.

She received endless compliments and felt beautiful, joyful, and vibrant. She reflected to me afterward that before this healing, she would never have considered wearing a sleeveless dress, ever. She had been so ashamed of her arms and her body, and she had felt a need to hide it, to shrink from attention. She had felt unsafe.

To wear a red dress that drew the attention of the entire room had been unthinkable.

And yet, there she was.

She took this red-dress energy into her board meetings and into her leadership at work. She began to get visible and speak up. She took up space in the room, with her body and with her voice. She was no longer afraid to command attention. She felt her input mattered—and it was now finally being received. She was able to be kind and compassionate toward herself, and this translated into other people being kinder and more compassionate with her. The "difficult" people on her team became less difficult. She was more effective as a leader, and she certainly enjoyed herself much more. The dread she used to feel about going to work was replaced with excitement.

The same red-dress energy carried over into her

relationship with her husband. They began to take vacations together—an indulgence that she had never allowed herself before, she was always working. Her husband remarked that they were able to have more fun together, and that he saw a spark in her that he hadn't seen in years.

I too marveled at Linda's remarkable transformation. Gone was the slumping, shrinking energy that expressed, *Don't look at me, don't listen to a single thing I say. I don't belong here. I don't deserve to take up space. I'm ashamed of my being and the way it inconveniences everybody. There is no room for me in this world.* Her new royal, queenly energy expressed, *I am a gift. My contributions are valuable. I belong here. I'm safe. I'm welcomed. I'm loved.*

FINDING THE HOLE IN THE FLOOR

Linda's work situation was the hole in the floor of her prison. As we began to dig, we opened up a tunnel to her jailbreak. Below the surface of her initial problem, we found layers of deeper trauma. Throughout our work together, we used embodiment practices to create safety, so that her prison guards could take a break. This allowed us access to deeper layers that had been unsafe to touch before.

As we discussed in chapter 1, the prison of PSD is constructed over the layers of ancestral, collective, and individual trauma. We tunnel through these materials as we make our jailbreak.

Welcome to everything you've been avoiding your whole life—numbing with food, alcohol, work, and the "comfort" of settling for less in your business or career and relationships, including your relationship with yourself.

The prison guards will continue to show up to defend each deeper layer. As we recognize them, we can return to the embodiment practices, like ones I shared in chapter 3, to establish safety. When the prison guards retreat once again to relax with their card game, we can turn back to our digging. Of course, this work is intricate, and there is a lot more that goes into it than I could possibly fit in the format of a book.

This part of the jailbreak journey is not meant to be traveled alone. We need qualified practitioners with the proper equipment—flashlights and excavation tools—to help us navigate in the dark tunnels of our trauma, and help us see the appropriate points to stop, rest, and ground ourselves in safety. On my website, you will find recommendations for finding a skilled embodied trauma resolution therapist.

If you're a therapist and are interested in learning more about the tools and techniques used in the jailbreak process and possibly adopting them for your own practice, you can find information about practitioner trainings on my website as well. One of the big frustrations for therapists and their clients is that trauma is not effectively healed with talk therapy alone. Many clients come to me with the erroneous belief that they had "worked through" their trauma—because they had been in therapy for years. With trauma, "talking through" does not equal "working through." Their bodies still carry trauma symptoms, that are still holding them back from being able to fully show up in their lives, relationships, and work as shiny authentic beings they are.

Most therapist trainings follow the patriarchal paradigm of being situated exclusively in the head and ignoring the body—as well as the larger context of human ancestral, collective, and personal traumas that I discuss in this book. Mine were too, for the most part. Following my formal education, I sought out opportunities to train with pioneers of mind-body trauma resolution. Over the years, adapting these tools in my work and personal practice and adding new techniques co-created with my clients—which I continue doing today—came together as the jailbreak curriculum. Now I make this curriculum available to people looking to heal and to therapists, through virtual and in-person trainings. You can learn more on my website.

THE PRIMARY WOUND OF PATRIARCHY

The primary wound of PSD for a woman is that of being worth *less* than a man. This is a core trauma that we all have inherited. A woman's body, a woman's ideas, a woman's life, her contributions in the world, her wants, needs, and desires—they're worth *less*. This wound is imprinted very deeply in our psyche.

It is such a dark place of despair that if we allow ourselves to go there and feel the full impact of this wound, it would be overwhelming. It requires us to feel not only the impact on our individual lives, but the impact of thousands of years of this wounding on billions of women. The prison was built to keep us from touching this wound. It was built on top of a deep dark slippery pit that is that wound.

This wound makes itself known in how much we sacrifice, how little we give voice to our desires, and how we struggle to get in touch with our needs.

The pain of not being able to have our desires met has separated us from them. The prison guards keep our desires locked up. Not being in touch with our true desires shields us from the pain of not having them met. A beautiful, sparkly, talented woman was sharing with me that she desired to create a partnership with a significant other. When I asked her, what she desired in her partner and relationship, she said, "I want him to be available. I want him to have a job." Knowing her, I would have imagined she desired to be adored in every way, ravished in bed, supported in all her creative endeavors by a partner who shared her thirst for adventure, who knew what it took to build and run a successful business, a man who shared her values, who was her equal in emotional intelligence, who deeply desired to commit to creating a lasting partnership with her—all of this or something even better.

When I pointed this out to her, she said, "But this doesn't exist. I want to be realistic." The intergenerational, cultural, and personal pain of not having her desires met, created defensive protections around it, the prison guards who say, "The partner you dream of doesn't exist. And if he does, he's not for somebody like you. I mean, look at you. You're definitely not at a "ten." A "four" maybe, on a good hair day. Gotta throw away those silly, unrealistic dreams and adjust your desires, darling. Or you'll spend the rest of your days as a crazy cat lady." And adjust her desires she did. Her "realistic" thinking, based on the "realities" of the PSD prison, has been shaping her life. She doesn't yet realize that there's a whole world outside of the invisible inner prison, where she can feel safe to be in touch with her true desires and free to create her own reality.

The bar for women's desires under patriarchy is set so low, because over the millennia, our desires could not shape our destiny. Desires were disruptive and dangerous. Women who followed their desires were punished. Ostracized. Excommunicated. Stoned to death. Burned at the stake. There's a lot of ancestral, cultural, and personal trauma that has poured concrete walls all around our wants and needs. To our subconscious, raising the bar feels like mortal danger. So the prison guards block our access to our true desires, and should they somehow leak out, they are swiftly neutralized by being labeled "unrealistic."

HOW ANCESTRAL TRAUMA MANIFESTS

I saw a clear illustration of ancestral trauma in a client of mine whose grandparents had lived through the Holocaust.

From the outside looking in, Amelia had never experienced anything that could be classified as "traumatic" in the traditional sense of the word. Amelia was in her late twenties, and by all marks she was doing very well in her life's trajectory. She came from a stable and supportive upper-middle-class family, graduated from a good school, and had built her resume through internships and volunteering. She was now successfully employed, making strides in her career, and in a loving, committed relationship. What's more, she was very confident. She believed in herself and knew her worth consciously.

And yet, at times she suffered from extreme anxiety and panic attacks.

If she had an appointment in an unfamiliar location, she would experience full-body panic and throw up. It took every ounce of her willpower to get on the train. She'd tried talk therapy and medication, and while these helped her cope somewhat, they didn't create a lasting effect.

When we discussed her family history, Amelia shared that her grandparents were Holocaust survivors, but she didn't feel their history affected her in any way. They had never talked about their experiences.

Yet the fears that were driving her anxiety were all

connected to unfamiliar situations, and many specifically involved taking trains to unfamiliar places—from an interview in the city to her boyfriend's birthday party at a bar in another suburban town. Consciously, these events have never conjured up for Amelia the images of Holocaust trains that were used to deport and transport the Jews to forced labor, concentration, and extermination camps. But her subconscious betrayed extreme fears connected to these situations—her severe anxiety was a manifestation of her system fighting for her life, for her survival.

In chapter 1, we covered some of the scientific evidence of genetic transmission of trauma, which suggests that at the root of Amelia's anxiety may be ancestral trauma. Traumatic experiences generate sets of survival instructions that are passed down in our DNA. The trauma of living through genocide created very strong survival instructions, which seemed to specifically highlight: do not take trains to unfamiliar places.

Although these fears were not "rational" from the standpoint of her life in the New York City suburbs in the 21st century, it made total sense that these survival instructions were operating in her subconscious. When I brought this to her conscious awareness, it allowed us to work through this trauma and release it. Amelia was finally able to board a train without her body being seized in a panic. She no longer needed to pick a seat close to the bathroom in case she got an urge to throw up. Amelia and her boyfriend even took trains all the way to Montauk—the farthest tip of Long Island—for a weekend getaway, and up through the Hudson valley, to enjoy the river and the foliage. Trains were no longer symbols of torture—they have become symbols of freedom for her: she is now able to go anywhere, anytime, at will.

This is the value of understanding and working with ancestral trauma. Looking through the conventional lens, Amelia didn't have any trauma that would register in a standard, therapeutic assessment. She was surrounded by a loving family, she was in a wonderful relationship, and financially secure. Her previous attempts to get relief from her incapacitating anxiety yielded cognitive-behavioral (CBT) strategies and a script for Xanax. Although these were helpful—like a bandage is helpful to stop the bleeding—over time these made her feel worse and affected her self-esteem. Her diagnosis seeped into her identity and began to erode her confidence and sense of self as a sovereign woman who could handle life.

Amelia felt like she was failing, because the CBT strategies were not stopping the overwhelming panic, and she was getting more and more reliant on the medication, which she hated. Ironically, the more she was trying to expand her world by going to new places, meeting people, and experiencing new things, the more her world was contracting, because to do so, she had to take Xanax. But it was not Amelia's failure. Remember what we discussed about the trauma hijack and the hindbrain that doesn't speak the language of words? Her CBT strategies involved analysis of the situation and changing the ways she thought about it and how she behaved. As you now understand, none of this is relevant at the time of trauma hijack. In order to even access the ability to analyze the situation, we need to interrupt the hijack first.

Another problem with this approach that does not consider the hidden trauma is that Amelia's anxiety was not based on her conscious thoughts and beliefs. Consciously, she knew there was nothing to be afraid of. Consciously, she believed she was capable, she was confident. It was her subconscious that was sending the signals of mortal danger through her system. So changing her thoughts with CBT was not exactly relevant, and a change in her behavior was not possible without interrupting the trauma reaction first. Without knowing all that, Amelia felt like a failure. Without an understanding of how ancestral trauma was affecting her, her therapist was aiming at the wrong target: trying to fix something that was not broken—her. Her amazing nervous system was working brilliantly to keep her safe, and her mind was already doing its best to manage this challenge.

So many women get medicated and stuck in the hamster wheel of coaching and therapy for years, trying to fix something that's not broken. Foundational to all our societal structures is the patriarchal gospel that we've internalized: *you're a woman, and therefore something's wrong with you, but not to worry—we have a pill, a corset, and foot binding to fix that.* When we see through it and look beyond it and consider the larger context that's affecting women's mental and physical health—the trauma that we've inherited and experienced as individuals and as a collective, that gets triggered daily—the "diagnosis," "prescription," and "course of treatment" change drastically.

And so do the results. Almost all of my clients have worked with therapists and/or coaches before discovering the jailbreak curriculum and have come to the conclusion that something was wrong with them—because despite their hard work, they still felt anxious, depressed, and stuck. They still couldn't relax without a glass of wine or a pill, could not lose weight despite grueling diets and punishing exercise, there was still disconnection and a lack of intimacy in their relationships, or they were still yearning to meet a partner who would be their equal, emotionally, spiritually, and financially.

One of the first things we do when we start working together, is take a guided tour of the invisible inner prison and examine the layers of ancestral, collective, and personal trauma that have been keeping her "safe" from living the life she desires. As we work through the layers of trauma, we tunnel out, and she walks free. But even until that happens, right now, every woman deserves to reclaim one simple truth that's foundational to the jailbreak movement: *there's nothing wrong with you.*

Feel these words reverberate through your body,

mind, and soul. Notice the prison guards raise their objections—say "Hi" to them and thank them for working hard to keep you safe. Use the Re-Power Tool to help the guards settle, then let yourself hear it again: *There's nothing wrong with you.* Deep breath. *There's nothing wrong with you.*

DIG FOR ANCESTRAL TRAUMA TO UNCOVER GIFTS

With each layer of trauma, we also open up a gift we've inherited. Our ancestors were amazing, remarkable people who accomplished incredible things. Their talents and feats are our inheritance, our birthright. The prison guards block our access to these gifts, and keep us from fully owning and embodying them, because the pain of the trauma closes that door.

Are you wondering what trauma and what gifts you might have inherited? Talk to your family, dig into your family history. A new discovery of my own jailbreak journey came out of a conversation with my grandmother.

My grandparents lived through World War II in Russia. They lived through extreme deprivation. They experienced the trauma of not having enough to eat, of not having heat in the extreme cold of the harsh Russian winter.

Though I did not have these same experiences, I have experienced these trauma reactions in my body, in this lifetime. My survival programming would start signaling with mild panic as soon as the temperature dropped from the 70s to the 60s, with trauma activation getting more intense as the thermometer reading descended. My relationship with food was also affected by my grandparents' trauma. *Eat more now*, my subconscious insisted, *because there may be no food later*. As a result, I would chronically overeat. I experienced an overpowering urge to eat at the sight of food, even if I had just had a meal. I yo-yo dieted for years, spent countless hours talking about it in therapy, and constantly struggled with shame and feeling like a failure, because while I was successful and accomplished in other areas of my life—I just couldn't get a handle on something so "simple" as eating appropriate amounts of food for my body's well-being. It was after I realized its ancestral roots and worked through the intergenerational trauma that this pattern peacefully dissolved. When we see the invisible, we can do the impossible.

When I began to heal these experiences, I also came into the inheritance of the amazing gifts I had received from my grandparents. Their resourcefulness: I too can make a meal out of nothing. My grandmother's commitment to her values: even during the war, with a famine going on, she would save up her rations of rice and bring them to the market to trade for some fabric so she could sew a new dress—honoring her value of creating beauty. They moved easily from one area of the country to another and abroad, integrating into communities where they didn't know anyone. They eventually settled in a city far away from their biological families and places of birth—because they thought it would be a wonderful place to build their lives. They established life-long friendships and created their "family of choice." They were adventurous, generous, fun-loving, and self-reliant.

When I was twenty-two, I moved from my hometown in Russia to New York City by myself. I didn't know anyone there. I didn't have financial resources. When people hear this story, they say, "This is so courageous, I would never be able to do that!" I used to think, *But it was so easy for me.* I fell in love with New York City and I decided to make it my home. I trusted that I would make it. Now, I recognize the wealth of the inheritance I'd received from my grandparents. It was those genetic instructions that gave me the ironclad assurance, self-reliance, and love for the adventure that most people would never even consider.

I'm eager to hear what ancestral inheritance you discover and claim! Would you please share with me? Send me a message on my website, www.drvalerie.com.

I'll be thrilled to hear from you. I'm constantly expanding my family of choice—calling all my fellow jailbreakers!

HOW COLLECTIVE TRAUMA MANIFESTS

After the 2016 election, where the first woman presidential nominee lost, my clients had changed overnight. For each woman, it seemed everything was an uphill battle. Symptoms of anxiety and depression became more prominent. These women had differing political views, and various assessments of Hillary Clinton's merit. But when Clinton was defeated, it reinforced the patriarchal cultural story for all of us: "A woman cannot be President."

These stories of worth-*less*-ness are inescapable in our cultural conversation. When we turn on the news or log on to social media, we're inundated with evidence of women's bodies and relationships being policed, women's choices scrutinized. In world news, we see countries where a woman cannot legally walk down the street without being accompanied by a man. Violence against women is so acute and present all over the globe. It is more overt in some places, and more covert in others. But each time we're made aware of the dangers, discrimination, and dismissals women face, our subconscious gets the message that the world is not a safe place. The invisible walls of the PSD prison get reinforced.

Many messages signaling *you're not okay* fly under the radar of our conscious awareness as normal parts of our cultural experience. In the commercial breaks we're served up solutions for compliance with the patriarchal prison code that assigns relative worth to women based on our appearance. "Anti-aging," "beauty," and weight loss industries depend on this compliance and perpetuate a cultural climate that reinforces it. This code punishes women for aging—showing signs of wisdom and maturity—or taking up space. Middle-aged and older women are featured in medication commercials. Women of color, differing abilities, or LGBTQ+ get only an occasional token nod to their representation in leading roles. The beauty "ideal" remains an able-bodied, straight, cisgender white woman with an adolescent body frame and twenty-something appearance—which the media reinforces daily.

Cultural messaging is insidious. I recently attended a conference that was all about new leadership models. They made an effort to have diverse voices in leadership represented, including women, people of color, and an anti-ageism presentation. The irony of the situation was that all diversity and inclusion and new leadership paradigm conversations took place underneath a huge banner representing the idea of leadership with a painfully familiar image: a handshake of two suited young white males.

These cultural messages continue to reinforce the status quo. Fighting this status quo is exhausting. It takes a toll on all women, and we can see it reflected in the casualties among women leaders. In 2018, the number of women CEOs of Fortune 500 companies dropped from its all-time high of 32 in 2017 to 24, with only one of them being a woman of color. Each woman CEO who left in 2018 was replaced by a man.[18]

Although there may be many causes of this rapid attri-

18 Claire Cain Miller, "The Number of Female Chief Executives Is Falling," *The New York Times*, May 23, 2018.

tion, here are some plausible ones that become visible when we consider the issue through the lens of PSD. The exhausting daily impact of microaggressions, the strain of operating in company cultures designed by men, for men, the uphill battle with bias driving women to work harder, faster, and do more—to prove that they're just as worthy as a man in this position, and PSD signaling to women through their subconscious wiring—*you don't belong here, it's not safe.* For women of color and LGBTQ+ women these stressors and the emotional labor involved in negotiating them are amplified. All this is a recipe for burnout, along with a devastating impact on women's health and relationships. Many women executives—colleagues and clients—have shared with me that all these experiences are a part of their daily realities. All these factors force brilliant, talented women leaders daily to step down from positions of power to save their lives and sanity—reinforcing the patriarchal cultural narrative: "A woman cannot lead."

We create adaptations to defend ourselves from the damaging stories our culture tells, and it takes immense energy to go against the defenses that keep us safely inside the status quo. This effort drains women leaders from the inside.

I attended a conference recently where several women took the stage to speak about women's empowerment. They were not professional motivational speakers—these were women in powerful leadership positions in big corporations. They said all the right things, and they were informative and inspirational in the content of their words, but emotionally, one after the other, these talks fell flat. Each speaker appeared on the stage with her shoulders hunched, her energy collapsed—as though to compensate for words that were too bold, each woman was trying to make herself smaller. I could feel the heavy burden of the stress of the daily struggle in their body language. Unfortunately, this nonverbal messaging has a subconscious effect of undermining the credibility of perfectly credible, capable, and accomplished women leaders. And the solution is not in "power posing"—the solution must reach deeper into our bodies, our nervous systems, to unload, process, and heal the hidden traumas that get triggered multiple times a day, conjuring up a chronic defensive-protective posture that's a tell-tale sign and but the tip of the iceberg.

HOW INDIVIDUAL TRAUMA MANIFESTS

Our bodies store the original imprint of whatever event caused us to feel unsafe. Our minds rationalize and tell stories about what happened, but our body memories are beyond stories. These memories are the record of impact, when we had a natural emotional response—be it fear, anger, hopelessness, grief, or even joy—that was interrupted.

Bernadette Pleasant, founder of the Femme! movement, whom I interviewed for my podcast *Her Success Radio* described an experience she had as a girl when she won an award at school.[19] The accolades were unexpected—she'd won against all odds—and she was bursting with joy and pride. She rushed home, excited to share the news with her mother.

Her mother suffered from depression, and this day was a bad day for her. When Bernadette walked in the door, it felt like all the air was sucked out of the room.

Instantly, without words, she got the message that there was no space for her joy.

There was no room for her accomplishment, no space for her bigness.

She swallowed her excitement, shut it down, and never shared about her award.

This is a traumatic experience of a different kind than what we have previously discussed: the trauma of frozen joy. I see this kind of trauma in every client, in every woman: Our big, expansive emotions are interrupted, we don't feel safe to be who we truly are in the moment, and we shut down those parts of ourselves that don't fit. We create adaptations that shape our lives to be smaller, quieter, less colorful, and less shiny than our authentic selves crave them to be.

---

19 Bernadette Pleasant, interviewed by Valerie Rein, "Empowerment Through Embodiment: From Shades of Beige to Bright Colors," *Her Success Radio*, February 14, 2019. Listen to the podcast at www.drvalerie.com/hersuccessradio.

IT MATTERS MORE THAN YOU THINK

I recently took part in a women's empowerment program in New York City run by Regena Thomashauer, aka Mama Gena, a feminist icon, founder and CEO of the School of Womanly Arts. In a room of 500 women from all over the world, Regena asked anyone who had experienced verbal, emotional, physical, or sexual abuse to please stand up.

The entire room rose to their feet.

Mind you, this was not a program for abuse survivors. It was a women's empowerment course that had brought together inspiring accomplished women from across the globe: entrepreneurs, creators, leaders.

As I stood surrounded by my sisters, the silence in the room was deafening. In this moment, every woman saw—likely for the first time in her life—that her very private traumas that she had hidden, dismissed as "not a big deal," "gotten over," "worked through" in therapy, or "succeeded despite of" were shared by every woman on the planet. There we stood, struck by this truth, each one of us a part of the ocean of women's suffering. We stood in this rare and precious moment—an opportunity to witness each other and be witnessed. We stood in solidarity with each other, in support of each other—and of ourselves. For the first time, our wounds were unwrapped from the bondage of shame and secrecy. And they did not diminish us. They brought us closer to ourselves, through embracing the truth of our experiences, and to one another—the sisters we didn't know we had.

Most women don't talk about their traumas. Some experiences are shrouded in shame, some are dismissed as "minor" events that a woman doesn't consider traumatic. Had Regena asked, *Have you experienced abuse?* Not that many women would have stood up. Understanding that, she helped women recognize their trauma by showing its many facets—"verbal, emotional, physical, or sexual." There are other types of abuse—mental or psychological (actions or words that negatively affect a person's mental health), financial or economic (controlling money or earning ability/access to opportunities), cultural or identity (isolating someone who doesn't speak the dominant language, threatening to "out" an LGBTQ+ person, or exploiting cultural/identity-based trauma, such as PSD, as a means of control). There are other types of trauma—medical trauma, bullying, community violence, disasters, complex trauma, early childhood trauma, intimate partner violence, terrorism and mass violence, refugee trauma, traumatic grief—among other life events and circumstances that leave scars. As you recall, we've defined trauma as *any event or circumstance that made you feel unsafe in your fullest authentic expression and resulted in creating trauma adaptations.*

Such experiences, each on its own accord and cumulatively, have lasting effects. The symptoms of trauma adaptations accompany us through our lives. There's a distinction to be made between the "big T" Traumas and the "little t" traumas of everyday experiences that inhibit the fullness of our authentic expression.

So many of our experiences are "little t" traumas. Think of when you got in trouble at three years old and your mother yelled at you. Or when your classmates made fun of you, or the time the teacher said, "girls don't act that way."

These little experiences are not knife stabs. They're paper cuts.

Each cut chips away at permission to be your fullest authentic self. Following these experiences, we subconsciously inhibit how smart, sexy, bold, and assertive we can safely be.

It's possible to bleed out from a million paper cuts. It's certainly possible to get an infection.

And yet, when women come to work with me, a very common thread of our discussions is that they disregard these experiences and don't consider them to be traumatic.

So many powerful, accomplished women I work with get trapped into thinking, *this shouldn't be affecting me, it's so minor. I should just get over this. It happened a long time ago.* These are the prison guards speaking. They keep us safe from being overwhelmed by our emotions. The prison guards rationalize these emotions away. They tell us, *it's not that bad.*

It was an unwanted sexual experience, but it wasn't rape. I was scared, but it's not like I was held at gunpoint.

These "minor" experiences culminate in ongoing anxiety, stress, trouble sleeping, or even depression. Because we never talk about them, never receive cultural validation of the damage they can do, we don't allow ourselves to consider that these may be areas in need of healing.

For some people, the prison guards' defense is along the lines of:

I am not a victim of these circumstances. I rise above them. I'm strong and won't let something like this affect me. I just get over it and move on. I don't let these things bother me. This is all victim mentality.

This rhetoric is, perhaps, the most dangerous of all. It creates a false sense of empowerment on the surface by cutting off the truth of the human experience and driving it into shadow, into shame and denial—deeper into the subconscious. Because the traumatic experiences are buried deeper now, there's very little to no conscious awareness of them—so the person is convinced that they are not being affected. But as numerous studies in cognitive neuroscience have shown, our behavior is predominantly driven by the subconscious. And if we can't see the invisible, we can't do the impossible.

Neuroscientist David Eagleman put it this way: "I think what we can conclude, is that if we have free will, it's actually quite a small player in this system because the way you make decisions has to do with the confluence of your genetics and your entire history up to this moment."[20]

John A. Bargh and Ezequiel Morsella call out the "conscious-centric" bias in our culture and psychology. They have demonstrated through review of existing research that "actions of an unconscious mind precede the arrival of a conscious mind—that action precedes reflection."[21] Let this sink in for a moment. *Action precedes reflection.* Science calls into question cognitive-behavioral, self-help, and personal development techniques based on the premise—founded on the conscious-centric bias—that changing the way you think will change your behavior and your life.

What happens in reality, is when traumatic experiences are ignored, denied, and even vilified under the guise of "self-empowerment," they continue running the show. So, contrary to the person's intentions, when they refuse to acknowledge these experiences and work through them, they truly become "victims" of these circumstances, that are now dictating their choices and behaviors without their conscious awareness or control.

Another rationalization the prison guards use is *I've dealt with this in therapy; it doesn't bother or affect me anymore. I don't think about it.* Now that you know that

---

20 Dave Blanchard and Carly Wyman, "Neuroscientist David Eagleman Studies the Subconscious," *Oregon Public Broadcasting,* February 18, 2015.

21 John A. Bargh and Ezequiel Morsella, "The Unconscious Mind," *Perspectives on Psychological Science,* June 26, 2008, 3(1): 73-79.

science has debunked the assumption that our conscious thinking is in charge of our choices and behavior (if your mind is still reeling processing this, I understand), you get how this prison guard defense is again based on a false premise.

What's more, as you already know, talk therapy doesn't reach into the embodied imprints of the traumas. An axiom in the mind-body trauma resolution field is that *your body is your subconscious mind*—which, as we've seen earlier, is actually in charge. Unless we dig down and investigate how these experiences play out on the level of our biology, our nervous system, we'll be forever chasing the tail of external expressions—thoughts and behaviors. It breaks my heart to know that millions of people go to therapy for years and take medication for anxiety and depression, but never truly heal.

A DOSE OF MY OWN MEDICINE

That's how the journey began for me too. I'd been in the mental health field for years, earned two graduate degrees in psychology, and through much of that time I never considered many of my own experiences to be traumatic—this was not what was taught in grad school.

Meanwhile, I had an emotionally volatile dad whose anger outbursts used to make me feel scared and power-less and a mom whose vortex of anxiety used to suffocate me, and, again, I felt powerless to get away from. Caught between these two patterns, throughout my childhood, I held my breath. Literally. I had asthma, and a lot of medical interventions around it. Growing up, I felt emotionally unsafe. Psychotherapy helped me understand that these experiences may be part of the cause of incapacitating anxiety and depression I'd felt. Years into talk therapy, I had all this insight in my mind, and all this anxiety and depression in my body. Insight did not change the way I felt, and I was a candidate for medication.

Luckily, I wound up in a yoga class, the one I kept walking out of, because I just couldn't tolerate the anxiety that came to the surface in the stillness of holding a pose. But eventually I made it all the way to the end and landed in the final relaxation pose, *savasana*. I had never in my life felt this. I loved that feeling of deep embodied stillness and peace. I began to crave that feeling. I got hooked on yoga. Yoga was my "gateway drug" in the world of mind-body healing. I followed the breadcrumbs into yoga teacher trainings at the Integral Yoga Institute in New York City and into studying with pioneers of mind-body healing and trauma resolution—Amy Weintraub (a leader in the field of yoga therapy who developed yoga protocols for depression and anxiety), Anodea Judith (a groundbreaking chakra psychology and mind-body medicine expert and somatic therapist), Jon Kabat-Zinn (mind-body medicine researcher and clinician, founder of Mindfulness-Based Stress Reduction), Zindel Segal (co-developer of Mindfulness-Based Cognitive Therapy alongside Mark Williams and John Teasdale) and many others.

On this healing journey, my body remembered the state of fear and panic I felt as a young child when my dad yelled. Now, as an adult woman, I realized that I would still experience that freeze when I felt aggression in the room. At the time, I was working in a corporate setting where a lot of aggression was present in meetings, and my response was to freeze. I was unable to speak up. Before recognizing my childhood experiences as traumatic and using the trauma resolution tools to heal their embodied imprints, I attributed holding back in meetings to shyness, introversion, or deference to authority instilled in me growing up.

Through mind-body healing, a life-changing shift happened: I was no longer hijacked by trauma in those unsettling situations. Instead, I was able to retain my presence, stay in my body, and speak up clearly and confidently. Given years of therapy that failed to change this pattern and my own ensuing conclusion that something was very wrong with me that even therapy was powerless to fix—this transformation felt nothing short of miraculous.

As I dove into working through layers of trauma, my authentic being finally began to unfurl. It finally began to feel safer and safer for me to step into my power and use my voice.

I wrote this book with the hope that it would help save

you years of searching for solutions for problems that are but the tip of the iceberg of trauma. Anxiety, depression, addictions, issues with sleep and weight, stress-related health conditions, relationship problems, challenges with creativity and productivity—I've seen all these improve and oftentimes fully resolve in my clients' lives, as well as my own, when we uncovered and worked on healing the underlying trauma. Trauma does not go away with time, because we have "moved on" or are "mentally strong." Through different symptoms, it's trying to get our attention. If we ignore it, trauma, like a child who's frustrated, gets louder. The symptoms proliferate or get more severe. Trauma—no matter how old—will make itself known. Because it requires recognition. It requires resolution.

When we pay attention and answer its call for healing, amazing things happen.

LETTING HIS HEART SING

Marcus spoke very fast, as if trying to outrun someone chasing him. Over the past three months he'd been having chest pains. He saw several doctors, got all the requisite tests, and was told that there was nothing wrong with his heart—that it was "just" stress. Yet Marcus's chest pains continued to intensify. His life was disrupted—he had trouble sleeping, he stopped working out. He woke up and went through each day feeling nervous and anxious.

His mind grabbed on to every news story of someone dying of a heart attack—to keep on stoking the fire of his anxiety.

We started by helping Marcus shift from being trapped in the head to moving into his body, using the Re-Power Tool. His speech instantly slowed down to what seemed like his natural pace. With Marcus out of the trauma hijack, we were now able to have a conversation.

After empathizing with his stress, chest pains, and fears of dying of a heart attack, I inquired about the bigger context of Marcus's life: What made his heart sing? What was his heart's desire? Marcus sat back in the chair, his face relaxing into a soft smile, as he began sharing with me his love for his fiancé Nicole and his passion for music. The more he talked about his relationship and music, the more he lit up from the inside. He shared that he wrote and sang his own songs, and his friends liked them, and he was dreaming of performing them for a wider audience, but—and his light began to dim once again—he was afraid to share them outside of his inner circle. And—he grew even darker—he was afraid Nicole would leave him, because he was scared to set the date for their wedding. And the reason he was scared to set the date—he continued, his voice getting constricted—was because he was afraid he would get fired. He had a demanding job as an investment banker. Lately, his anxiety and frequent doctors' appointments were causing severe interference with his work. He couldn't concentrate, he was making mistakes, he was irritable with clients and colleagues. As he was sharing this, Marcus's breath was getting shallow and he was starting to feel chest pain again.

I thanked Marcus for sharing and asked him to check in with how the fears felt in his body right now, to get in touch with the sensations of fear. Marcus reported that he felt extreme constriction in his chest.

Instead of going back into his head, where he would once again be at the mercy of anxious thoughts, I invited Marcus to stay in his body. Instead of fighting the constriction (and have it fight back and intensify), I asked him to make space—lots of loving and accepting space—for the fear. Marcus was surprised yet willing to experiment. He noticed that he was able to stay with the sensations of fear, and it gave him a feeling of control. As our experiment went on, Marcus also noticed that fear hadn't escalated into panic, like it normally would.

I then asked Marcus to inquire, with curiosity and without judgment, what the sensations in his chest were all about. I specified that this was not an intellectual inquiry. I instructed him to drop the question right into the area where he was feeling the constriction and to listen to his body respond. I gave him a tip: The response may come in a form of an association, an image, a sensation, a memory, or inner knowing, intuitive sense. And when he gets it, I noted, the original sensation would shift.

Marcus followed my instructions earnestly. He was

so exhausted from the weeks and months of doctors' appointments and medical tests. Conventional medicine had left him out of options, so he was now open to something new and out of the box. After a couple of minutes of quiet introspection, Marcus said in a quiet voice: *I fear failure. I fear I'm not good enough for her. I fear my music is not good enough. I fear I'm not good enough for my job.* He dropped his face into his hands in shame.

I celebrated Marcus's discovery and asked him to feel into his body again and allow the physical sensations—that now spelled out shame rather than fear—take him to the earliest memory when he first experienced that shame of not being good enough. I guided Marcus in a practice of connecting with his inner child—to feel, heal, and release that trauma.

He was able to connect with his inner boy and offer safety, comfort, love, and acceptance to that part of himself that had been locked in the trauma of being shamed for too long.

As this experience integrated over the next days and weeks, I taught Marcus a couple of breathing techniques to counteract his anxiety and regulate his nervous system. Each technique took two to three minutes, and Marcus practiced them regularly at work and at home. He rapidly saw the results. His chest pains became less frequent and less severe. He felt in control of his physical state, which helped him to feel in control at work. His focus and productivity were improving. He smiled again and joked around with his clients and colleagues. They remarked that it was good to have the "old Marcus" back.

In his spare time, Marcus began posting his songs on YouTube—for people outside of his inner circle—and received great feedback. One day, he shared with me that he had been asked to perform his songs at a party. At this point, only a few weeks into our work together, his chest pains seemed like a distant memory. Marcus looked and felt healthy. He was able to sleep through the night again and wake up rested. He resumed working out. He was glowing. He had bigger news to share: he and Nicole had set a date for their wedding.

As you saw in Marcus's story, trying to solve the issue on the level of symptoms was not working for him. When we took a closer look, we discovered a single root to all of his challenges—a traumatic experience that's so common and thus so easy to dismiss as "it happened a long time ago," "it's just life," "everyone goes through it," or "man up!" Following the embodied imprint of this traumatic experience allowed us to recognize and resolve it. And the symptoms followed suit.

The symptoms were the messengers of trauma, calling his attention to an area that needed healing before his life could expand. The constriction he was feeling was the shell of the old patterns of hiding and avoiding (which by now you may recognize as trauma adaptations or prison guards)—the patterns that were not congruent with his heart's desire. They had to go and give way to the life of his dreams. Marcus's body successfully got his attention through the messengers of the symptoms. Once the message was delivered, received, acknowledged, and acted upon, there was no longer a need for the messengers. They could go on leave.

Without attending to the message, Marcus's worst fears might have become a self-fulfilling prophecy. These prison guards were trying to make sure that he didn't experience what was not congruent with the subconscious story of "I'm not good enough" imprinted from his childhood trauma of being shamed. So they were causing conflict in his otherwise happy relationship, undermining his performance at work, and making sure that people didn't hear his music—because to those traumatized parts, all of this seemed too good to be true, and had to be sabotaged—to avert the risk of failure, being exposed as not good enough, and to protect him from feeling shame.

Once Marcus released that trauma, not only did his symptoms go away, but more joy and creativity flowed into his life than he had been able to access before. This is my favorite effect of mind-body trauma healing work. Once we unlock the channels that trauma has blocked, we can have uninhibited experiences of pleasure, excitement, and creative flow.

COMPLETING THE STORY

These different types of trauma—ancestral to collective

to individual—layer over each other. We may be triggered by an individual experience that connects us back to ancestral or collective trauma. Or we can experience these traumas layering the other way: an ancestral or collective trauma could create conditions and events in our lives that trigger personal trauma. Our nervous system responds to each of these events, and the body stores memories about them to keep us safe from future harm.

We can return to these body memories of trauma and complete the experiences that didn't get a chance to be completed at the time. Our bodies can release traumatic imprints when we establish safety to complete these interrupted emotional expressions and meet the needs that were not met at that time. Such as, feeling trapped and unable to run away from a situation, or feeling so angry but being unable to express your anger, or so excited and having to suppress it. When we complete these experiences—actually running away, fully expressing our anger, embodying our exuberant joy—we can have this appropriate response witnessed and received appropriately. When we're not punished for our expressions, but celebrated, validated, and acknowledged for them, we experience healing.

Having a witness to our fullest expression is key to healing, integrating, and releasing our emotions linked to trauma. Much of what we are trying to deal with as our "personal problems" are not true personal problems. We were born with these responses in our DNA, and they were trained into us from the collective culture. Trying to solve them as personal problems doesn't work, because these were not problems created in isolation. Thus, they cannot be solved in isolation.

We receive wounds in community, with the participation of other people—and we create healing in community with the participation of others. Throughout our lives, we received distorted reflections of ourselves, from people around us who didn't see the truth of us—because they could not see clearly through the walls of the invisible inner prisons of their traumas, while our own prisons kept quite a few authentic parts of us safely hidden. To heal these wounds of distorted perceptions and the resulting mistaken identity requires standing in our truth and being seen. We collectively built the old story, the prison story. Now we need to collectively build the new freedom story as we step into our authentic power. We need a supportive community to reclaim our ability and willingness to be vulnerable.

I have found in-person retreats invaluable—both on my own healing journey and the ones I facilitate for my clients. When our individual healing journeys converge, we discover that the collective power and genius of the group is so much greater than the sum of its brilliant parts. We also discover that whatever deep secrets, whatever pain tightly wrapped in shame we've been holding on to as proof of what's wrong with us—that all others have been holding on to theirs, and they are remarkably similar if not identical.

When we access these forbidden experiences, express these forbidden emotions, and speak up about these forbidden things while being witnessed by supportive others, we are healed through their understanding, compassion, love, and acceptance of us exactly as we are. In expressing our authentic selves, we can connect to others who have felt the same way. Many women who have been in retreat together say it was the first time in their entire lives that they felt so safe to show up authentically and be seen, heard, upheld, celebrated, and loved. Many life-changing breakthroughs have emerged from these experiences—of allowing themselves to be welcomed and embraced in their full expression and creating this sacred opportunity for others.

BUILDING A BRIDGE INSTEAD OF DIGGING THE TUNNEL

It can be so tempting, particularly for high-achieving women, to skip this step of digging the tunnel, and instead build a bridge over their trauma. We identify the prison guards, spot a weak link in the defense, and do a Hail Mary pass right on through—skip straight to the final step of jailbreak covered in the next chapter—mastering the game of *how good can it get?*

Building bridges on the shaky foundation of unre-solved trauma is a bad idea from the engineering standpoint—sooner or later, they collapse. Another prob-lem with this approach is that there is so much gold that we miss underground. Wrapped in defenses that protect painful experiences are also disowned parts of ourselves associated with them. All the parts that feel "not enough" are there in the dark. All the denied, forbidden, and vilified parts such as our anger, our sexuality, and our insatiable needs and desires. The parts that feel "too much" are there too—our bigness, brilliance, our power—things that people around us were uncomfortable with, and as a result, reflected back to us in distorted images from their funhouse mirrors. For many women, owning our beauty and enjoying truly loving and reverential relationships with our bodies and ourselves is also down there in the shadows.

These disowned parts of ourselves remain in the subconscious and hold power over us until we discover and integrate them, so we can have a conscious relationship with them and, part by part, reclaim our authentic wholeness. Each time we cross the bridge, trauma gets triggered, and our subconscious sends up the trolls to collect tolls: stress, irritability, conflict, isolation, anxiety, depression, inflammation, headaches, backaches, self-sabotage—a steep price to pay for the bypass.

Since we have to dig the tunnel, we bring to the process safety, community, and the "power tools" of rewiring the nervous system and cultivating capacity for pleasure and joy. Each new layer reveals more access to our authentic expression and our fullest life.

EXERCISE: SHAKE IT OUT

As you dig into these successive layers in the tunnel, each discovery will come with its own emotions and its own energy. One powerful and simple way to move the energy of emotions through your body is to shake. Shaking is animal discharge 101: In nature, when a deer survives a wolf attack, it gets back up and shakes all its limbs to reset the nervous system. Similarly, when aid workers go to war-torn areas, one of the first things they do to help a group move through trauma is to gather together and shake. It's a helpful tool that transcends language barriers, and as people come down from that, they are more relaxed and more open because their system has discharged. By shaking, we express and complete the fight-or-flight response that our bodies feel when we are stressed.

EXPANDING OUR EMOTIONAL RANGE

Trauma makes us physically shrink, constrict, become smaller. It makes our breathing shallower and narrows the range of our authentic expression. Trauma interrupts the natural flow of emotions, and unprocessed emotions get "frozen" in the body, over time accumulating and interfering with the natural flow of our energy, restricting our access to our emotions, and constricting their range.

As our ancestral, collective, and individual traumas cause this constriction, they dictate which emotional expressions are unsafe. It is unsafe to be too exuberant, too loud, too brilliant, too excited, to show our grief, our anger, our ecstasy, our pleasure. We show up in an ever-narrowing emotional range. It makes people feel disconnected from themselves and others, less alive; it underlies a lot of relational discord, anxiety, depression, and addictions.

With little use, our full capacity to experience deep, authentic emotions diminishes. We are not used to the experience of moving the energy of these emotions through our bodies. When we do that, when we move the stuck emotions of grief, rage, joy, or any other expression deemed unsafe, we make room for flow once more.

With this increased ability to conduct our emotions and our energy, we tap into greater abilities to conduct our authentic power.

MODALITIES FOR EMBODIED TRAUMA RESOLUTION

Simply talking about trauma doesn't resolve trauma. Trauma is in the body, which remembers these experiences even if the conscious mind does not. It's important to bring together mind, body, and spirit in trauma work.

For more information, I recommend great books written by the pioneers of this field: *Waking the Tiger* by Peter Levine, and *The Body Keeps the Score* by Bessel van der Kolk.

Many practices and approaches have stemmed from this work, and new methods continue to be developed.

What they all have in common is that they work directly with the body's intelligence. First, it's important to create embodied safety to access experiences of trauma. Then, it's possible to transform those experiences on the physical and energetic levels, as well as the level of the mind.

It's important to choose a practitioner with whom you feel comfortable. A note of caution: When we work with a therapist, there is a danger of giving away our authority and power to someone who "knows what to do." I have fallen into the trap of trusting therapists' interpretations over my own inner knowing.

As you select a practitioner to work with, consider how comfortable you feel speaking up and whether you feel heard. Request a phone conversation or even a personal meeting before hiring the person to see whether you resonate with them.

If your intuition raises any red flags or objections, listen to it. Your intuition will not lead you astray. Don't let your rational mind override its messages. This is a big part of our healing from PSD: we reclaim our power not only by listening to our intuition, but by acting on what she tells us.

Intuition is binary. It tells us YES or NO. There's no rationalization or elaboration—those come from the mind, and those are not what you're looking for. When you are comfortable with your practitioner, you'll know it. Do your research, gather information, but let your intuition make the final choice.

At www.drvalerie.com I've included resources to support your search for the right practitioner for you.

CHAPTER FIVE

SAVORING FREEDOM

When she designs, and then lives, her own destiny, a woman naturally sets right everything wrong in our world.

—REGENA THOMASHAUER, *PUSSY: A RECLAMATION*

WHEN JESS CAME TO SEE ME FOR THE FIRST TIME, she was tightly wrapped in anxiety. She had a list of what she wanted to talk to me about. She clutched that piece of paper like a lifeline.

Jess was a bright, attractive woman in her 30s, and her list was indicative of her type-A, high-achieving personality. Top of the list of her concerns to address was that she felt she was running out of time to meet her ideal partner and have a family.

She'd had a string of challenging relationships behind her, and in each one she had tried so hard to make the case that the relationship was workable and that it would get better. If only she tried a little harder, she would make it work.

To me as an outside observer, it was clear that the men she was attracting were not on her level. Jess valued her career, her ambition, and her education. She worked out regularly and led a healthy lifestyle. These men did not. None of them had gotten their lives going in any kind of direction. They didn't value family or health and didn't have career ambitions.

The panic of running out of time, the prison guards whispering: *You're in your prime now, it won't be like that forever. You're aging. Look at these wrinkles. The expiration date of your shelf life on the market is in sight. Stop being so picky. You're not all that. You'll be lucky to have any halfway decent guy stick around. Are you throwing away perfectly good candidates because you're not willing to give them a chance? Don't expect a Prince Charming to show up, your perfect match made in heaven. You gotta work on your relationship to make it work!*

Sound familiar?

These guards pushed Jess to jump headlong into each of these relationships and invest much more than her partners did—in desperation and hope against all hope—until she had a trail of heartbreak and failure that "confirmed" what the guards had been telling her: *I can't get any halfway decent guy to stick around. I must be aiming too high. I gotta lower my standards, or I'll be alone forever, a crazy lady with eight cats.*

These were her actual thoughts. Before she knew these were the voices of the prison guards, she believed that these thoughts were "the truth," because they were based on the "evidence" of her relationship failures.

These thoughts tormented her day and night, pulling her deeper into the vortex of anxiety. She was not sleeping well. Her eating became disordered: she was restricting calories, because if only she dropped a few pounds—according to her prison guards—her "market value" and her chances of finding a suitable mate would increase. Her exercise routine became punishing and compulsive—there was no joy in it; it was a weapon in her war on her body, on herself. Meanwhile, her weight was already on the low side of the range that would be considered healthy. She had trouble focusing at work. She was becoming more and more reclusive—her interactions at work were tense, challenging, and conflict-ridden. Outside of work, she had pretty much shut down her social life.

You know by now that this is how PSD operates. The prison guards don't want us to aim high because the wound of worth-*less*-ness has programmed into our subconscious the idea that we don't deserve it. Our thoughts and actions and how we feel about ourselves reflect that subconscious programming. We aim low so that we don't get hurt by not getting something that, according to PSD, we can't get.

Of course, we get hurt a lot worse by the prison guards

that keep us from going after our true desires—and even knowing them. We shrink and wither. We make ourselves smaller than we are, trying to fit into the suffocating corset of the PSD mold: *don't shine too brightly or you'll be burned at the stake.* Or in the classic words of my mother, "No one would want to marry you."

As I'm sure you've figured, the solution to Jess's relationship problem was not lowering her standards but raising them. Her relationships were doomed from the start, because she was attracting men who resonated with her shrunken, corseted, foot-bound version. These men didn't have the capacity to embrace her big and shiny authentic self. The authentic parts of her would rebel, sooner or later, demanding to be seen and loved for who she truly was. But here's the rub: Jess was not showing up as who she truly was. So, in order to have the internal permission to aim higher and attract the same caliber of person, Jess had to recognize and embrace her big and shiny authentic self first.

I see so many high-achieving women stuck in this same predicament without realizing it. The reason being that consciously, they know their accomplishments and their worth. Jess did too. But her subconscious programming did not match. She needed to reclaim her inner preciousness on a deep, embodied, cellular, energetic level. Until then, this subconscious programming of little self-worth kept playing itself out, creating plenty of opportunities to gather "evidence" to validate, confirm, and reinforce it, through self-sabotage in her relationships, health, and career.

After working through the bigger frame of PSD, we dug into Jess's childhood experiences and uncovered that her family did not reflect her worth to her. Her mother had not been attuned to her needs as an infant and would leave her crying and would not attend to her. As a child her feelings had been consistently invalidated and not given space to be heard.

This is the case for generations of people, raised by parents who bought into the cultural beliefs at the time, that attending to children's needs would "spoil" them, foster "dependence," and render them "weak" and "unfit to handle life." It's not these parents' fault: they were doing their best. But the unfortunate outcome is generations of people who haven't developed the capacity to be with their emotions, because they haven't learned it from their caregivers. As a result, we have an epidemic of addiction to substances, food, work, TV, shopping, and prescription medication, among other things—as go-to, culturally-accepted means of dealing—or, rather, not dealing—with emotions.

Many of us, like Jess, did not receive an appropriate affirmative reflection of our full authentic being growing up. Our "imprisoned" caregivers operating within an "imprisoned" culture were only able to reflect to us what they could accept. And they could only accept in us what they could embrace in themselves. Everything else got denied, ignored, or rejected. This is the imprint of our being that we took with ourselves into adulthood—pre-shrunk, to fit the patriarchal factory mold.

For Jess, the layers of PSD and personal trauma of neglect, had imprinted a story in her: *If my needs cannot be met, why bother trying? I have to settle for whatever I can get.* She knew she couldn't get more attention from her mother, and she settled for whatever crumbs of affection she could get from this foundational relationship. As a result, for the rest of her relationships, the table was set for the familiar—not for a feast, but for the crumbs. Jess's system was not prepared to handle a feast, it couldn't digest it, and it would have rejected it.

We began by empowering Jess with mind-body tools to manage her anxiety and help her befriend and inhabit her body. This helped build her capacity to be with her emotions and enabled us to work on healing these early childhood experiences and reclaiming her worth from the PSD wound of being worth *less* as a woman. Amazing things began to happen.

Jess began recognizing her needs and desires. She learned to attune to her needs in the way that her mother could not. She started finding out what she really, truly deeply craved, and she began to bring those experiences into her life. She joined social groups and went on active outdoor adventures. She created art—a joy she had forgotten a long time ago.

She shifted her attitude toward exercise. Her fitness

routine was no longer driven by self-hate. She got off the hamster wheel that millions in our culture are trapped in—exercising to "look good," but never feeling good about the way we look. From a self-punishing activity, Jess's exercise routine transformed into a source of joy, pleasure, satisfaction, and practice of self-care and self-love.

Jess was training her mind-body system to take in, digest, and metabolize more joy, happiness, and love, as she was setting the table for a feast.

HOW GOOD CAN IT GET?

Little by little, Jessica began experiencing herself as an attractive woman—not intellectually or through artificial "confidence"-building hacks—and this shifted something very deep in her. She was able to show up in her pleasure and her joy. Her anxiety about running out of time resolved.

She met a man who was very different from the men she used to date before.

This man was attuned to her needs, just as she was now attuned to them. He was interested in what she was interested in. He desired to support her in what she wanted to do and give her exactly what she craved.

At first, this freaked her out.

Jessica was not used to a relationship that felt like this. She couldn't bring herself to take a bite of this delicious dish—it looked too good to be true, what if it got taken away? Her prison guards were sending her messages and making elaborate plans to sabotage her relationship, to keep her safe from the pain of disappointment and heartbreak.

He's going to leave me as soon as he finds out who I really am and where I come from. My family is so messed up, I can never introduce him to them. His family is so loving, I can't get attached to them, I can never be like them and a part of that world. Jess would discuss with me plans for never letting him see all of her...Maybe they would never move in together? Yes, that seemed like a perfect plan. Except, if they didn't, he would eventually want to move on, because he would want a "normal" relationship with a "normal" girl so he could have a "normal" family, like his. She could never give him that, because she's not "normal" like people in his world. She should probably just break up with him now, before they get too attached, and save them both the heartbreak. *Yes, that's it,* she'd think, *I'm gonna talk to him tonight.*

Every time she shared these self-sabotaging thoughts and plans with me, I felt so grateful that we were on this journey together. We were able to look the prison guards in the face, acknowledge and thank them for trying to keep her safe. We then would interrupt the trauma hijack and help her ground in embodied safety. We would inquire what the prison guards were protecting her from and follow the answers into healing the underlying layers of trauma. The jailbreak process enabled Jess to allow for this wonderful expansion in her life.

Jess and her guy did move in together. Petal by petal, she did allow him to see the authentic fullness of her. He did not run for the hills. The more her authentic being unfolded, so did his love for her and the strength of their relationship. His family and friends embraced her as "the best thing that's ever happened to him." She embraced them back. They got married.

When we emerge from tunneling out of the prison, we're tasked with learning to savor freedom. Our eyes need to adjust to the bright light and vibrant colors of the world on the outside. Our system needs to learn to digest, assimilate, and metabolize the delicious feasts that life has prepared for us. The energetic channels that had been blocked by unprocessed trauma, now cleared and open, need to strengthen and dilate to run more energy of the full spectrum of authentic emotions. Our whole being gets recalibrated to the new reality—as we unlearn the game of *how much can I bear?* and master the game of *how good can it get?*

As Jess dropped the old game of checking the boxes of the prison "success" scorecard of how much she should weigh, by what age she should start a family, etc.—as she was no longer at the mercy of her subconscious programming running her life from the control centers of trauma—she was now free to consciously create her life, designed by her desires. Jess began drawing new blueprints for her life that she had not gotten from her family or society. She was constructing mutually supportive, fulfilling relationships in her partnership, her self-care, and her career.

THE NEW GAME

Like Jess, we all have our set of familiar survival instructions that keeps us from reaching for more in our lives. When we begin to reach, we begin to run into the prison walls.

Our mothers and grandmothers may not have known the walls were there. Success, financial independence, and choosing our own partners in love were not necessarily on the menu for women even a few generations ago.

We are the pioneers in jailbreak.

There are no blueprints, no role models, no rules. We're not following our mothers', grandmothers', our ancestors' lives any longer. We are not in Kansas anymore. We are in uncharted territory.

To break out into the dizzying light outside the prison is exhilarating, overwhelming, and disorienting all at the same time.

When we heal the trauma that underlies our captivity, we begin to crave expansion. We want more joy, more impact, more visibility, more financial power. These are no longer tokens to earn us conditional love and approval that they were in prison. These spring forth from our deep, authentic desires unfurling into the light, breathing full breaths of freedom, running bigger and bigger volumes of life force through our system, and feeling unstoppably greedy for the full expression through creation and experiences. This is what it feels like when we shift from survival to thriving.

Thriving is not the absence of anxiety and depression or restoring a normal sleep pattern and stress levels. This is neutral. Thriving happens when we remove the invisible inner barriers to our fullest authentic expression. When it feels safe to have all our true colors shine forth. When this feels non-negotiable and normal. At this point, you may or may not have a reference for what this feels like. Thriving only becomes possible as we jailbreak.

Remember that the skillset of thriving is not the one we inherited. Generations after generations before us mastered the skillset of surviving. Theirs was the game of suffering, the game of *how much can I bear?*

The new game is the game of thriving. It centers around the question, *how good can it get?*

Playing this new game requires a new toolset that we make from scratch. In order to create our lives by conscious design, we need to be in touch with our desires. This is where we begin.

We awaken our pleasure—she who took a bite of the patriarchy-poisoned apple and fell asleep millennia ago—and follow her to the secret and sacred places only she knows the way to, to uncover our authentic desires.

SYSTEM UPGRADE

In order to get in touch with our desire, we need to open our channels of emotional expression.

In the last chapter, we saw how trauma limits us to a narrow emotional range. With embodied trauma resolution, the channels that conduct these emotions open up, and we are able to move more emotions, energy, and power through our system with ease.

So often I see high-achieving women who exercise their power without healing intergenerational, collective, and personal trauma. It takes a huge toll on their systems to be in the public eye, to play full out in the fields where men have had a historical advantage—not only in opportunity, but in being believed in. Being believed in is one of men's unconscious privileges.

Women face a lot of the visible and invisible resistance from the patriarchal status quo—from logistical barriers to microaggressions, as well as our own subconscious programming stemming from PSD and other traumas, that's working against us.

As a result, the energetic demands on successful women's nervous systems are enormous, but their systems are not prepared or trained for it. Our systems are patterned after our mothers' and grandmothers', but the demands on them are overwhelmingly, undeniably, unignorably higher. Our biology has not caught up with our opportunity, and it's killing successful, accomplished women. It's like entering a Formula

One race driving a Toyota Corolla. We give our all to the race, and we complete on par with men, but our engines overheat and our vehicles fall apart. I believe this to be one of the hidden reasons behind the burnout epidemic among high-achieving women, including the recent rollback in the number of the female CEOs of Fortune 500 companies. Thankfully, there's a solution—a system upgrade.

The more fully we experience life through all our senses, the more all our faculties click into full power. We can play and perform at our highest levels. Our creativity, productivity, and inner guidance becomes available to us. We experience serendipity in the way we are able to see and seize opportunities.

Congratulations, jailbreaker: You now have a beautiful track in front of you. You just need to upgrade your vehicle. You're entitled to claim a luxury race car of your choice. You can do it by rewiring your system that was trained for survival and giving it a thriving upgrade.

PLEASURE POLICE

Remember the prison guards? Those trauma adaptations that kept you in check inside the invisible inner prison? In this step of the journey, as you're leaving behind the old prison game of *how much can I bear?* and mastering the new game of *how good can it get?* you'll encounter resistance in the form of pleasure police.

Pleasure police control how much good you're allowed to experience. These are internalized enforcers of the patriarchal prohibition on pleasure.

Like prison guards, pleasure police are not bad guys. They too serve an important function. You see, over the millennia of little use, our capacity to experience pleasure has drastically diminished, all but atrophied. The energy channels to run our pleasure and power have withered and weakened. For us to plug in fully and suddenly turn the dial from one to ten is risky. Our nervous system can get overwhelmed.

Back in New York, when my family and I moved into our mid-century modern home, the electrical system was original, circa 1962. When we started plugging in modern appliances, we kept blowing the fuses multiple times a day. We could only plug in an electric kettle *or* the hair dryer. This problem continued until we upgraded the electrical system in the house. Our bodies operate much the same way: when we run the increased energy of our pleasure and power through a system that has not yet been upgraded, we risk overwhelming it.

For a deeper explanation and illustration, I turn to yogic teachings on *kundalini* awakening. *Kundalini* is a Sanskrit term that describes life force, the energy and consciousness that is coiled at the base of the spine. When yogic practices lead a practitioner to liberate this dormant energy and it starts running through the channels, it can overwhelm the system and a practitioner may experience a crisis that may manifest not only spiritually, but in mental and physical health symptoms.

Pleasure police enforce the pleasure speed limits, which is helpful for the safety of our journey. As we heed their reminders, we are pointed in the direction of where we need to increase our capacity, open up subconscious permission to experience more power and pleasure as well as the energy channels to receive and run this life force at a greater volume and rate. Then we can safely raise the speed limit. As our vehicle becomes upgraded, we can run faster, safer, and have exponentially more fun playing big in the world without inviting a burnout or a crisis.

EXERCISE: CONSCIOUS EMOTIONAL EXPRESSION

To open up and strengthen our energy channels, we first need to clear them of stuck emotional energies of interrupted, uncompleted, and unresolved emotional experiences. This exercise is designed to support you in exploring this process.

Emotions are raw and primal. Think how a toddler expresses their frustration with a full-bodied tantrum. Their ecstasy, too, is full-bodied. My daughter used to do a brilliant full-body pout when she was disappointed. Her head and shoulders would collapse, her arms dangle lifelessly, and her feet would shuffle and stomp at the same time, as she walked down the hallway, making her disappointment and disapproval known.

One of the practices that can support you in expanding your range of emotional expression is invoking your inner toddler.

It can be helpful to create playlists of music to help you tap into your emotions. Create a playlist that brings out anger, another that takes you to sadness, and one that invokes joy.

First, prepare a space that allows you a full range of motion. Roll a yoga mat or a rug on the floor and surround yourself with cushions and pillows. Carve out a space that gives you full permission to feel your emotions as they arise.

Play with expressing whatever emotion is present for you right now.

Express it through movement and sound. What does your body want to do with this emotion? In what ways does your body want to move? What sounds do you want to make?

Remember, you're not the present day you—an executive, a leader, a business owner, for whom this exercise may feel silly and a waste of time. Let your two-year-old self have a ball with it. Give her 100 percent permission to do her full-bodied anger, sadness, and joy routines. (An added bonus: this is one of the best "anti-aging" practices I know.)

Each emotion has an embodied "signature" for how it typically expresses in your body. The signature of anger, for example, may appear as a clenched jaw, tight shoulders, and a flush of heat. Use this exercise to observe and learn more about your embodied emotional signatures, so you can more easily identify and work with them consciously when they come up, as opposed to them driving the bus from the subconscious.

To express anger, you can have your face show it, squeeze your fists into tight balls, stamp your feet, bare your teeth, and scream. (Loudness does not matter as much as permission to reclaim your voice and make any sound at all—so please be gentle on your vocal cords—you'll still get the full benefit of this practice.) You can smack or throw the pillows and cushions around you.

The emotion of anger usually has a root of grief and sadness underneath it. As you feel the energy of anger move through, become sensitive to how the quality of that energy wants to transition.

To express sadness, you can hold yourself and howl and rock back and forth. Roll around on the floor. Crawl, as the sadness feels heavy and slow and pulls you closer to the earth. Don't overthink it—let your body move herself. The first time you do it, she may feel timid and shy, not sure if she has permission to express herself—as it's been taken away years ago. But bringing yourself back to your two-year-old-self wisdom may help break the spell.

As you keep your attention on the sensations that are arising from the body, feel how the energy of sadness may want to transition again. Welcome this transition by calming and comforting your nervous system. Run your fingertips across your face. Run your hands down your arms with some reassuring pressure. Give yourself a hug. Caress other parts of your body that call to your awareness.

Once calm and peace set in, the playground is set for joy. Play that happy song, do that silly, crazy, happy dance. Start saying "Ha-ha-ha-ha-ha-ha-ha" until you break into a nice bout of belly laughter. No "laughing like a lady"—laugh your tail off like a respectable two-year-old would! Laugh through your face, ears, neck, shoulders, arms, hands, fingers, chest, belly, back, butt, vagina, hips, legs, feet, and toes! Have every cell of your body join in the symphony of joy.

In this exercise, you may find that some emotions are more difficult for you to connect with than others. For women, anger can be a particularly difficult emotion to access fully. If you can't connect with a particular emotion, express that emotion for someone else. If you can't connect with your own anger, for example, connect with the anger your mother couldn't express, or your grandmother, or your friend, or even a fictional character on your favorite show. Do it for them. As you explore a full range of expression, you will be clearing your emotional channels.

Much of the energy of our emotions can be moved through our bodies in a matter of seconds, and it becomes easier the more we practice. According to research in neuroscience, the lifespan of an emotion in the body and mind is ninety seconds.[22] You can complete this whole exercise in about six minutes.

Why should we "waste time" on conscious emotional expression? For the same reason we "waste time" on flossing. Through the "flossing" of moving e-motions (unlocking the emotional energy trapped in the tension in our bodies and minds and setting it in motion), we prevent unwanted material from accumulating in our system, decaying, causing stress and leading to emotional pain that not only we but others around us would feel. Moving through these full ranges of emotional expression is like flossing. When we don't move our emotions consciously, they move us through our subconscious—and rarely in the direction that we want to go in.

The hardest part of this practice is recognizing when we need to do it. The second hardest part is actually giving ourselves permission to do it. We're usually the last one to notice that we're pent up. Our family and coworkers feel it before we do—that we're irritable, short, impulsive, unfocused, disconnected, and not fully present. Because when we're hijacked by trauma, caught in prison guards' stories, and carried away by overwhelming emotions, we're not exactly in our most

22 Jill Bolte-Taylor, *My Stroke of Insight*, New York: Penguin, 2009.

conscious and aware place. So it's wise to practice these emotional expressions regularly, in a controlled, safe environment, regardless of whether or not we feel we need it. Just like flossing. With practice, our channels to move these energies remain open and clear and we are able to be more present, connected, focused, and loving—as our family and friends may attest to.

It will feel very weird and awkward at first. Most likely, you're not going to want to do this practice by yourself. I encourage you to connect with other people and opportunities that allow you to consciously express your emotions. We create a deeper experience when we gather together to feed off each other and support each other.

That's why I hold retreats for women jailbreakers to practice together. For this exercise, we gather in a circle and face away from each other, so that each woman feels connected and supported by collective energy, as well as safe in her own personal privacy and not worried about being judged. Following the practice, women often share how healing the experience was for them—to have permission to express their anger, sadness, and joy without being judged, punished, or rejected for it. It is beautiful to witness a simple practice like this begin to melt decades of women's self-censoring, self-judgment, and feeling wrong and not-belonging.

Additionally, you can integrate emotional expression into

conscious movement practices, such as dance or yoga, to encourage your emotions to express through your body as you move. Put on music that helps you tap into a particular emotion you wish to explore and take your body's lead on how she wants to move.

TAKE TEN

With our channels of expression open, we are able to take in more sensory detail from the world around us. As we develop awareness of our sensual experience, we are able to slow down and be more fully present in the moment. More than that, we can specifically slow down to milk every experience for the pleasure it contains, to nourish and energize us and support our re-calibration from the game of *how much can I bear?* to the game of *how good can it get?*

If you find it challenging to slow down and take in the pleasure, you're in good company. Neuroscientists have shown that humans have "negativity bias": negative experiences register in no time, while most positive experiences are readily dismissed as non-essential for survival. Rick Hanson and Rick Mendius explain that the brain is "hard-wired to scan for the bad, and when it inevitably finds negative things, they're both stored immediately plus made available for rapid recall. In contrast, positive experiences (short of million-dollar moments) are usually registered through standard memory systems, and thus need to be held in conscious awareness ten to twenty seconds for them to really sink in."[23]

In other words, it's survival of the anxious.

Positive experiences are not deemed essential for our survival, but they are essential to thriving. To effectively shift from the old survival game to the game of thriving, we need to practice a new thriving skillset. For example, consciously engaging the brain circuitry in recording positive experiences—and taking at least ten seconds at a time to be present with them through the senses to make these pleasure imprints powerful and lasting. When used consistently, this practice becomes a powerful tool in mood management and preventing depression.

Mindfulness-Based Cognitive Therapy, one of the treatment modalities that I'm trained in, is an eight-week group training program shown to be more effective in preventing depression relapse than the traditional approach of talk therapy and medication.[24] One of the powerful practices that the MBCT protocol uses is paying attention to and tracking positive experiences. I appreciate this practice, because it directs participants to pay attention to the embodied experience—not only the cognitive one. In my work, I've further developed this exercise, integrating the neuroscience findings regarding the time threshold

23   Rick Hanson, PhD and Rick Mendius, MD, "Buddha's Brain," *WiseBrain.org*, 2007.

24   Meagan B. MacKenzie and Nancy L. Kocovski, "Mindfulness-Based Cognitive Therapy for Depression: Trends and Developments," *Psychology Research and Behavior Management*, 2016, 9: 125-132.

it takes to imprint positive experiences. I instruct my clients to stay with each experience for at least ten seconds—longer, if possible. My clients report rapid and lasting positive shifts in their mood, energy, resilience, and overall outlook, including shifting to embrace new opportunities more readily and feeling more connected and fulfilled in their relationships with themselves and others, in their work, and other aspects of their lives.

PLEASURE MINDFULNESS

A traditional mindfulness practice, like we saw in chapter 3, involves experiencing the present moment through the senses. We open to what we can see, hear, touch, smell, and taste, and these sensual details allow us to connect to our environment directly through the body, as opposed to through the filters of cognitive concepts and interpretations.

It's the difference between eating a scrumptious meal and licking the menu. When we're up in our head versus the body, we don't engage with our actual experience in the present moment—we don't actually taste the delicious meal and get nourished by it.

It's not our fault. Trauma keeps us locked in our heads and we don't habitually experience our reality through the body, through the senses. As a result, our lives are chockful of neutral and pleasurable moments we miss and don't get nourished by. Whereas negative experiences continue to register and pile up with no conscious effort on our part and drain our resources. These negative experiences form a reference library of survival which our experiences get filtered through—when we're living in the head versus in the body—and as a result, our experiences get skewed toward anxiety, negative outlook, disconnection, and depression.

Consider the unremarkable experience of going from your front door to your car. Mundane occurrences like this happen on automatic because the mind is conditioned to use the minimum input to get us from point A to point B. On survival setting, the mind is an efficiency machine. But if we want to thrive, we need to shift from just getting from point A to point B to actually experiencing and enjoying the journey.

Jon Kabat-Zinn, a pioneer of the mindfulness movement in the West whom I had the pleasure of learning from, put it this way: "Mindfulness means being awake. It means knowing what you're doing."[25]

Life serves up an amazing banquet of mouthwatering dishes every day, but the mind is only interested in reading the menu, deciding in advance, based on the past experience, if the dish is going to taste good or bad, ticking off the things it's had before. *I've seen this tree before. I've had this meal before. I've slept in this bed before. I've taken a shower before. I don't need to pay attention to these—*

---

25 Jon Kabat-Zinn, *Wherever You Go, There You Are,* New York: Hatchette Books, 2005.

instead I'll use my capacity to track potentially threatening experiences.

To the senses, everything is new. You've never seen this particular tree, in this particular light, at this particular moment on this particular day before.

To the body, each moment is lived, real, and fresh. The more we bring awareness to the sensation of the bedsheets against our skin when we wake up, the smell of soap, and the warmth of the shower, the more we're able to taste the deliciousness of that moment.

Coincidentally, studies on mindfulness suggest that the practice helps us experience pleasant experiences as more pleasant, and unpleasant experiences as less unpleasant.[26] This may be explained by the mind's role in dismissing the positive events as non-essential for survival and elaborating on the negative ones, drawing from the reference library of prior painful experiences. When you stub your toe, you experience not only the pain from your body, but the spinning of your mind that goes, *oh my God, I'm so clumsy. It hurts so bad. I hate this couch.* Engaging with our experiences through the senses serves as an antidote to this toxic interference, and it helps us minimize the filtering effect of the mind that amplifies the negative and downplays the positive.

If you want to shift from licking the menu to enjoying a delicious meal, mindfulness is your friend. In the jail-

---

26   Kirk Warren Brown and Richard M. Ryan, "The Benefits of Being Present," *Journal of Personality and Social Psychology,* 2003, 84(4): 822-848

break curriculum, we take mindfulness benefits a step further to help us counteract the negativity bias of the mind and increase our ability and capacity to be fueled and nourished by the pleasure of daily experiences. Note: the following practice is a part of step five in the jailbreak system—if you run into resistance or don't feel you're getting the benefit from this practice, this may indicate that more work is needed in the first four steps.

EXERCISE: PLEASURE MINDFULNESS

Start by noticing any experience that gives you pleasure in this moment. It could be as simple as feeling a smooth, warm cup of tea in your hands. It may be stepping outside and feeling the sun on your skin. It may be eating a delicious meal or taking a bath.

Experience this moment through all five of your senses, as best you can, for at least ten seconds. Give your system the time it needs to imprint the experience in your internal reference library.

From there, the next step of the practice is to ask yourself, *how can I enhance this pleasurable experience?* There are two ways to do it.

First, you can open up more permission to experience pleasure. What more could you take in with this moment? How long can you stay here? What else do you notice?

Second, you can adjust something in the moment to make it more pleasurable. Is there a shift you can make in your chair to get more comfortable? Would it feel good to take a deeper breath, or drop your shoulders? If you're in the shower, adjust the water temperature until it's exactly right. Turn your music up or down to the exact volume you want. Get closer to the things you want to see in more detail. As each adjustment makes your experience more pleasurable, continue to soak it in for ten more seconds.

When you begin to develop an awareness of what is pleasurable, you can create "pleasure triggers." What textures and scents appeal to you? What sights and sounds hold your attention? As you identify the common objects and elements that you enjoy in your daily life, you can use them as sensory amulets: they become touch stones that help you practice anchoring your awareness in pleasure and receive nourishment it brings on demand.

THE PROGRESSION OF PLEASURE

We start the pleasure mindfulness practice with experiences that are naturally pleasurable. We then go a step further and turn our attention to neutral experiences.

Is there something pleasurable you can find in getting the mail? Bring your awareness to how you feel in your body as you walk to the mailbox. You might notice that your feet feel particularly comfortable in your shoes, or the light is shining in a way that gives you pleasure. Maybe you enjoy the texture of the paper in your hands. You can bring pleasure to mundane moments and enhance your experiences following the same steps.

When we have developed our practice and skill of bringing pleasure to neutral experiences, we can bring pleasure mindfulness to unpleasant experiences. Perhaps being in a dentist's chair makes you feel nervous and uncomfortable, but you can bring your attention to the sensations that increase your comfort. Maybe the temperature of the air is comfortable, or the sensation of your back being supported by the reclining chair, or you may enjoy the minty smell and taste of the mouthwash.

By bringing awareness to any sort of pleasure in the midst of an experience that's not inherently pleasurable to you, you can shift from a stress response to a relaxation response, from contraction to expansion, from survival to thriving.

Remember, these practices are taught in step five of the jailbreak curriculum. It is important that you've built the "muscles" that enable you to shift from "unsafe" to "safe," before you can shift from "safe" to "pleasure"—and "more pleasure."

The more we practice, the more we calibrate our inner radar to track pleasure in everything. This has a domino effect that allows us to not only experience more pleasure in the moment, but to expect pleasure. For example, when we expect a "yes" response to a proposal, even if it ends up being a "no," it's more likely to land for us as "not yet" or "something even better is coming"—and it doesn't take wind out of our sails. This also trains us to consciously adjust our experience in the direction of asking and receiving more and make requests that create greater pleasure. In other words, pleasure mindfulness can transform your life.

ASKING FOR WHAT WE WANT

When my client Megan began practicing pleasure mindfulness for the first time, her pleasure police pushed back in a very predictable way. *This isn't necessary,* they said. *What are you doing? This is a waste of time.*

Because she knew how to work with them, she was able to practice anyway. She started with simply noticing simple things, like what gave her pleasure when she was drinking a glass of water. She realized she wanted a slice of lemon in it. She wanted to drink out of a fancy glass. She promptly upgraded the glassware.

Then she began noticing more things. Every day, her family came home before her, and when she came home from work, there was still a dishwasher full of dishes to unload. She would unload the dishwasher, set the table, and put dinner on the table.

She realized that this scenario was not giving her optimal pleasure, and for the first time ever, she asked her family if they could please unload the dishwasher before she got home.

They were all too happy to help. Megan was completely puzzled.

This small thing had been such a thorn in her side for years. Every day she came home to a dishwasher full of dishes, her mood would plummet and her mind would start replaying the story: *They don't care about me. I'm invisible to them. What's so hard about unloading the dishwasher? If they gave a damn, they would do it.* But she never actually asked them to do it, because based on the reference library of negative experiences (some her own, some inherited) about what, as a woman, she's entitled to, she was expecting a pushback. So, why would she ask and put herself through a humiliating and disheartening "confirmation" of her story—that her family doesn't care about her? That, as a woman, it's her job to take care of their every need? That she's not entitled to be taken care of?

To make sure you don't get the wrong picture, let me clarify that Megan is no shrinking violet. She's a lioness. She's the breadwinner in the family, a powerful executive who's known for her direct, no-nonsense communication and management style at work. Why then, at home, would she hold back?

It turns out, Megan is in good company. In her book, *When She Makes More,* money expert Farnoosh Torabi cites research that shows that in heterosexual marriages, women who make more money than their husbands actually do more housework than wives who make less or about the same.[27] By now you're well aware that it's not women's fault—PSD drives them to overcompensate for playing way outside the zone where women were traditionally allowed to perform. All of these choices, as you now know, are driven by our subconscious. You're probably making some you're not aware of right now, that keep you playing smaller than you are and tolerating things that suck the life out of you. I keep discovering my own PSD adaptations hiding in plain sight all the time.

When I brought this one to Megan's awareness, she was puzzled by how long she had been living in the story and the experience that was not in her pleasure and never questioned it. Because she already had a pleasure mindfulness practice, she was able to make a request to her family not from a place of frustration, from the old game—*what's wrong, and how do I fix this?* Instead, she asked from a place of pleasure of the new game—*what's right, and how do I enhance it?*

When we communicate from a wounded place, we tend to blame. *You're responsible for making me feel this way.* This kind of communication, which stems from trauma, disconnects us from ourselves and others. A wounded communication might have looked something like, "I can't believe you guys. I work so hard, such long hours,

27 Farnoosh Torabi, *When She Makes More,* New York: Avery, 2014.

I'm exhausted, and then I come home and you can't even be bothered to unload the darn dishwasher. I can't believe how selfish you are." Et cetera, et cetera.

Sound familiar?

Instead, Megan's communication came from a place of connection. "I'm so excited to have dinner with you guys. I'm putting together a nice meal for us. You know what would help us have it faster, and help me relax and enjoy time with you, is if you unload the dishwasher before I come home. Would you do that?"

In this pleasure-based communication, she speaks to their value and their contribution, so that she can be more relaxed and enjoy their time together better. In place of guilt and shame, it brings acknowledgment and appreciation. Instead of conflict and disconnection, it creates closeness and connection.

A word of caution: This is not a surface-level "communication training" hack. Nor is it a "fake it 'til you make it" trick. None of the strategies in this book are. If you put a frosting of sweet communication over a layer cake of decades of resentment and anger, it will still taste like crap.

When we truly shift to operating from a place of pleasure and joy, people can feel it in the energy of our being. They want us around more. They listen to us more. They cooperate. They want to fulfill our requests, made from a place of pleasure, for things that would create more pleasure for us. It gives people pleasure to give us pleasure.

But we need to establish ourselves in our pleasure first to show them the way. Our partners deeply desire to give us exactly what we need. They just need our leadership. They need us to let them know exactly what will give us pleasure. For that, we need to be in touch with our own needs and desires—which, as we've seen throughout this book—takes a moment to get to through the layers of PSD defenses.

This pleasure-begets-pleasure principle applies not only in your intimate relationships, but in every situation you can imagine. Most of the time, people are so disconnected from their pleasure in the moment, and that sends a message to other people that their presence and contributions are not being valued and appreciated.

I remember the first time I conducted a pleasure experiment at a restaurant in San Diego. I followed my pleasure to ask for the waterfront table, even though as a solo diner I was initially directed to a less desirable one. I was in my pleasure, which showed in my relaxed, happy, and appreciative energy and communication. From that place, I continued to make my requests. For a blanket to keep me cozy. For wine samples to pick the one I would enjoy the most. My old story prison guards showed up to assure me that I must be annoying the server, that I was being "difficult" and "demanding" and other words typically used to describe a woman who asks for what she wants. Yet I stayed in my pleasure. I leaned back in my chair, my legs stretched out and resting on another one, wrapped in a blanket. I was savoring the breaths of the salty ocean air, the bites of my scrumptious meal, and the sips of the delicious wine. When the server came to pick up the check, he said, as a warm smile lit up his face, "It was *such* a pleasure to serve you today."

As I was getting ready to leave, I looked around the gorgeous upscale restaurant patio, and was struck by the dissonance between my internal state and that of the other diners. They had the same ocean to enjoy. The same fine cuisine and wines. They had company to delight in. Yet their faces reflected anything but pleasure—they were scrunched by worry, detached, lost in thought. Not a single face was lit up and relaxed by the inner pleasure glow. In that moment, I realized that being in my pleasure brought value to the world. That it was anything but selfish, indulgent, inconsequential, irrelevant, or inconveniencing others.

On the contrary. My pleasure was broadcasting the energy of my appreciation of others and the world around me, and that frequency was contagious, and acted as a powerful antidote to the cultural dis-ease—the status quo of stress, anxiety, and disconnection. This is the game of survival, that people continue to play under the most luxurious of circumstances. Because the outer circumstances don't free us from the invisible inner prison of trauma. It's only the inner work and healing that creates the jailbreak that enables us to truly thrive—under any circumstances.

THE SOCK DRAWER THAT ENDED MY MARRIAGE

A warning: pleasure mindfulness can be hugely disruptive to your life.

Not long after my ER episode, I began practicing pleasure mindfulness to help me reconnect with myself, with my authentic desires. The practice prompted me to rearrange my sock drawer. As I sorted through the socks, I had a stunning realization: Most of the socks I owned and regularly wore I didn't enjoy. In fact, I hated the feeling of these socks on my skin. *Why do I still have these?*

I grew up in poverty in the Soviet Union. Socks did not get thrown out even when they developed holes. My mother and grandmother darned them, and I received sock darning lessons as a little girl (pro tip: use a wooden darning mushroom; in a pinch, a light bulb will do). To get rid of socks because they did not *feel* good was heresy.

This discovery was my first glimmer of awareness of what I was tolerating in my life. When this domino fell, it created a ripple effect of awakening to other parts of my life that didn't feel right and didn't bring me joy. I realized what I had been tolerating in my marriage. Deep fundamental things that years of marital therapy and heaps of best intentions on both our parts had failed to resolve.

When you weed out what you're tolerating, you will open up space for new things. Organizing a sock drawer ended my marriage. It also opened space for a life that would light me up, where I won't feel like a dead woman walking. I began to design a life of joy and deep connection that I desired. Never before awakening to my pleasure had I dared to admit to myself that I didn't have what I desired. Just like my client Jess and so many women clients, friends, and colleagues, I had "worked on" my relationship for years.

My PSD conditioning underneath it all had pre-calibrated me for the game of *how much can I bear?* versus *how good can it get?* in my marriage. Marriage was not supposed to be a source of pleasure and exuberant joy for a woman. So I didn't expect mine to be. My husband was a really good person and a great dad, so my prison guards convinced me that this was enough, that I was not to be greedy, that I was not allowed to want more. Their rationalizations were so convincing: *Every couple has their problems. You have to work on your relationship. So many great women are single, is that what you would prefer? As a forty-year-old single mom, you'll never find a partner, let alone a good one.* But the moment I pulled on the thread of a hateful sock the whole thing unraveled. I was faced with the truth: I wasn't happy. I hadn't been happy in years. I wasn't miserable. I was dead inside. Our daughter deserved a mother who was alive, connected, vibrant, and happy—yes, happy! I dared to desire to be happy.

My husband and I had the conversation that had been coming for years. He, too, felt exhausted from incessantly "working on" our marriage without any results that would be satisfying for either of us. The bitter resentment that had built from both sides was creating a toxic living situation for both of us and our daughter. We amicably decided to part ways.

I'm not a proponent of divorce. It's the last option that I considered in my own marriage, and that I would ever consider with my clients. I live for the transformations in relationships of the couples I get the privilege to work with. It is incredible to see people fall in love again and become intimate after years of a sexless marriage, to see them light up in each other's presence after years of stone walling, toxic arguments, and resentment. This transformation takes both partners connecting with, understanding, and working through their hidden traumas—together and separately. It takes two—more often than not, with the help of a skillful guide—to jailbreak a relationship.

ON GUILT AND SELFISHNESS

Women are not used to attending to what makes us feel good and brings us more joy and pleasure. When we dare to think about our own needs, the prison guards jump into action. We feel guilty, selfish, and in the wrong. *How dare I pause to smell the flower, when I could be doing laundry? How dare I be so ungrateful as to want more? My life is good. Am I tempting fate?*

These prison guards are keeping women in check, making sure we comply with the PSD prison code of conduct that spells out what a woman is entitled to and what she is not. As each prison guard shows up, we go back through the steps of using the Re-Power Tool and other techniques that help us hop off the trauma time machine and return to the present moment, into our body. We thank the guards for keeping us safe, and watch them settle back to their card game, so we can proceed to reach for our desires, uninterrupted. This enables our nervous system to shift from signaling "unsafe" to "safe," which is a necessary precondition for opening up to pleasure.

This often plays out in the bedroom. For most women, sexual activity is fraught with triggers that hijack their nervous system into a trauma response. Their bodies feel unsafe, but their minds try to rationalize and override it—*I love him, this should feel good, what's wrong with me?* Then they have an experience of pain during intercourse, or trouble with arousal and orgasm, and according to the PSD instructions, they blame themselves. If this is your experience, I encourage you to practice the tools for establishing safety before you can open up to receiving pleasure. There may be trauma to work through before pleasure becomes fully available to you, and I suggest seeking help from a mind-body trauma resolution practitioner. As you get help for yourself, don't forget your partner, who needs to better understand your needs and may benefit from their own trauma healing. I offer my suggestions for finding and selecting a practitioner on my website.

As you begin to dip deeper into pleasure, you'll realize what a counter-cultural move that is. Our culture drives us to live in our heads and not in our bodies and if you're a woman, to ignore your true needs and authentic desires. For a quick demonstration of how this cultural conditioning manifests, take a look at your schedule: How do you give away your time? Do you prioritize yourself last?

Here again, I do not recommend any "hacks," "fixes," or "fake-it-'til-you-make-its," because they backfire. Like going to the spa but spending the entire time thinking about your next meeting or what's for dinner.

None of what's marketed as "self-care" helps you to break out of prison. A jailbreak moment is walking out of the grocery store and feeling delight in the beautiful food you're taking home, the soft breeze, the quality of the light. When your cells feel alive, when you take a deep, luscious breath, and feel amazing in your body—regardless of how your clothes fit or the number on the scale—*that* is a moment of jailbreak.

I have seen women take their businesses to the next level by following the breadcrumbs of pleasure. They begin to notice how pleasure-impoverished their schedule or task lists are and get on a mission of reclaiming joy in their work. They shift their focus to the activities that bring them pleasure—which incidentally happen to be in their zone of genius.

In *The Big Leap*, psychologist Gay Hendricks writes about the leap one takes from their zone of excellence to their zone of genius.[28] For myself and my clients, I find that jailbreak makes the leap possible, effortless, and inevitable, because it activates a woman's authentic genius and makes that G-zone magnetic. A woman's zone of pleasure *is* her zone of genius.

When we let our pleasure guide us, we find ourselves at our peak performance. We're at our most productive, our most connected, and our most creative. We're at our best as leaders, because our presence and our energy is inspiring and motivating to all around us.

Trauma keeps us in a reactive state where we keep sacrificing and suffering. We keep doing things that don't bring us pleasure, playing the game of *how much can I bear?* and when we have nothing left to give, we either explode or implode. We pick arguments or we isolate. We engage in trauma reactions of fight, flight, and freeze, and nobody wins.

When we jailbreak and master the game of *how good can it get?,* when operating from a place of pleasure becomes our new normal, we are grounded in clarity about what we want and we communicate it in a skillful way that brings joy to us and others—and effortlessly wins their cooperation. These communications revitalize our relationships at home and at work.

I have seen my clients shift their team cultures and skyrocket their revenue because they were fully able to engage in their zone of genius. Which required following

---

28 Gay Hendricks, *The Big Leap,* New York: HarperOne, 2010.

the steps of jailbreak from *unsafe* to *safe* to *pleasure*. Similarly, their personal lives have been transformed: they've become closer with their kids, and the long-forgotten sex lives with their partners returned juicier and richer than before. When we lead with pleasure, people resonate and respond with their own pleasure and gratitude.

ONE STEP AT A TIME

The process takes care of itself when we begin where it is easiest. That's why we start with tasks that are inherently pleasurable, then shift to neutral experiences, and finally tackle the unpleasant ones. Building your pleasure capacity in this way is like building a muscle. You can't show up to a gym for the first time and press a hundred pounds. You start with five-pound weights and work your way up.

Similarly, you can't jump straight to an unpleasant task and imagine you'll "fix" it by bringing pleasure. You first have to build up a reservoir of pleasure inside yourself by engaging with inherently pleasurable, and then neutral, stimuli through pleasure mindfulness.

I've got great news for you: This process is designed for multitasking. Infusing any activity with pleasure helps you stay in your body, in the present moment, which helps your effectiveness, productivity, creativity, and connection in any task and situation. Additionally, when you bring awareness to one particular part of your experience, your enjoyment has ripple effects out to other areas of your life. Experiencing more pleasure nourishes your nervous system and counteracts stress, which, again, has very positive ROI at work and at home.

Attending to our pleasure is not just about our mindset, but about building our physical capacity to move the energy of our experiences through our system. We're slowly upgrading our vehicle on the racetrack, so that we can generate more speed without wear and tear on our bodies and minds.

Your jailbreak will happen in cycles and phases. You will have moments of pure pleasure, and then something will come up, another aspect of trauma will get triggered and activate its own prison guards. Huge congrats! Each time this happens, it's not a rollback. It's not a shortcoming. Despite what the prison guards have to say about it, you're not failing at your jailbreak—you're rocking it! The more stuff gets triggered and brought up from your subconscious to your conscious awareness, the more leverage and control you have in your life. The more opportunities you get to heal trauma, the more you shift from the old game of *how much can I bear?* to the new game of *how good can it get?*—and the stronger you become as a conscious creator of your life experience and circumstances. The jailbreak system and tools are designed to support your journey every step of the way.

CHAPTER SIX

RELATIONSHIPS ON THE OUTSIDE

Be the change that you wish to see in the world.

—MAHATMA GANDHI

IN THE MID-1950S IN THAILAND, WHILE MOVING A plaster statue of Buddha from one location to another, the movers made a wonderful mistake: they dropped the statue.

When they looked closely at the damage they'd done, they saw something shining from the crack in the plaster. The statue was actually made of solid gold. The Golden Buddha was, and still is, the largest solid gold statue in the world. A few hundred years before, it had been covered over in plaster to disguise and protect it from invaders.

Finally, with one crack, its true nature was revealed.

That story stayed with me. There was something in it

I needed to understand. Then one day in a session with Eleanor and Keith, who were struggling to relate to each other, the story came back to me like a bolt of lightning.

It was suddenly so clear to me what was going on with them. They both loved each other so deeply—and deeply is the key word here. They were reaching for the gold inside of each other, but it was covered in so many layers of defenses, so many layers of clay built up and molded over their gold.

I shared the story of the Golden Buddha with them, and they both teared up. They recognized in a flash the armor they had been carrying around for years and years. They had been stuck communicating clay to clay, defense to defense—which was the source of their disconnection, ongoing conflict, and dissatisfaction in their relationship. Beneath that, they were deeply longing to relate to each other gold to gold—to experience themselves and each other in their full shiny authenticity, vulnerability, and realness. This realization was the start of their beautiful story of transformation that we witnessed in chapter 2.

As we embark on the jailbreak journey, it is important to bring our partners along as allies in our work. Very often, a woman who gets on any personal development journey feels a deepening gap between her and her partner. This gap can create a lot of friction as she tries with the best intentions to get her partner to read the books or attend the seminars that she finds helpful. It can feel to the partner like she's trying to "fix" them.

I did that for years in my marriage. I wish somebody would have shown me a different way.

Having learned from my own mistakes—and having been my own most challenging client—I understand now that what we need as we jailbreak are tools to feel safe in communicating our needs to our partner, and to help our partner feel safe.

This communication takes place from deep vulnerability. It's important to move through the steps of jailbreak first to create safety. Trying to get to vulnerability before we feel safe to do so backfires: You may go deep and share what you feel but get re-wounded if you haven't built up internal resources to navigate that terrain. When that happens, the human animal inside gets re-traumatized and hides deeper. More clay is put on top of the gold. This is often a side effect of couples therapy that is not trauma-informed and does not use mind-body trauma resolution tools.

But when you use the jailbreak tools to create deeply embodied safety, you can feel strong in your vulnerability. When the human animal inside feels safe, she doesn't need to run, fight, or play dead. This strength comes not from defense and armor, but from true empowerment from within.

You can show up naked, without your armor or weapons, and speak your truth and be open to receive your partner's input, whatever it is, without shutting down. That is true empowered vulnerability that you can access when you learn to work with trauma.

When both people in a couple can truly feel safe with each other and connect from a place of empowered vulnerability, the problems that used to be unsolvable get solved in an instant. It turns out that when a couple speaks to each other from their most vulnerable place, they can see that they've wanted the same thing all along.

SPEAKING CLAY TO CLAY

Most problems in relationships are driven by clay to clay versus gold to gold communication. The message we communicate gets distorted through our own clay—through our defenses—and when our partner receives it through their clay, it's distorted even more.

It's a very broken game of telephone. By the time the message gets through, it's something completely different.

I saw this in action when a couple, Amy and Ben, came to see me. Amy had been the primary breadwinner of the family, in a very successful corporate position, and she was looking to start her own business following her own mission and her higher calling.

Ben had been a stay-at-home father, and now the kids were grown. To support Amy's mission, he would need to go back to work. They were both scared. Amy had tried bringing up the idea before, but Ben had shut down. He wouldn't talk about it.

He was happy with the way things were. She was desperate.

When they came to me, we did a few practices in embodiment to create safety and help them move deeper in their communication. They moved from talking clay to clay to talking gold to gold.

From that place, Amy was able to share her hopes and dreams. She shared very vulnerably how she was feeling: she was dying at her current job and drawn to live a bigger life that allowed her to share her gifts in a whole different way.

Ben met her in that vulnerability and responded from his own. All this time, he said, he had been scared. He didn't know how to support her. He was scared for her, and whether she was making the right move. He was scared for their family, and his ability to provide for them. Because he never knew how much it meant to her, he didn't engage. Now that he heard her, he was the one to bring it up. To Amy's surprise, Ben volunteered that he would be happy to start looking for a job, so he could provide a reliable income and she could make the big leap.

Previous to this discussion, he had not heard her through the clay. The message he had received was something along the lines of, "I'm not sure what to do next and I need your support." It wasn't clear to him what this meant, and it triggered his fears and defenses. What did this mean for their marriage? *Is she talking about leaving me? She says she's unhappy, but what can I do? Will I be able to take care of her? What is going on?*

Her vulnerability allowed him to lower his own defenses. When Amy was able to clearly express what she wanted, Ben now had an opportunity to support her in the way that she needed. It was something he'd longed for, as had she.

As we orchestrate our own jailbreak, we need support from our partners and close relationships. The way we relate to others—our partners, our children, our parents, and friends—shifts post-jailbreak. We need to remember that more often than not, we're relating to people who are still in their own prison cell as we're learning to navigate the world of unlimited possibilities outside.

It's important to understand what our partners' prisons may look like. Our collective culture doesn't just imprison women; it dictates what is "okay" and "not okay" for everyone, and it decorates men's prison cells quite differently.

CONDITIONED MASCULINITY

A Google search pulling from different sources reveals a definition of masculinity as the possession of qualities traditionally associated with men. Muscular. Driven. Aggressive. Rugged. Strong. Robust. These "traditional associations" emphasize just one side of the spectrum of what it means to be a man.

Just as patriarchal culture has narrowed what is acceptable for women, for men it has locked away qualities not deemed as "masculine." Men are conditioned to repress and disown qualities that are ascribed as traditionally female, like being kind, emotionally expressive, connected, empathetic, and—most especially—nurturing.

It is deeply traumatizing to men to grow up and live in a culture that denies the full spectrum of their humanity and pushes into the shadows so many beautiful qualities they all possess.

Because patriarchal culture doesn't support men in fully expressing their nurturing, connected, empathetic, and deeply emotional nature, this collective trauma creates armoring around those qualities. *Boys don't cry. You're acting like a girl. Don't be a sissy.* This creates what author, educator, and activist, co-founder of A Call to Men, Tony Porter calls "the man box"—the invisible inner prison that patriarchy has built for men.

A man's natural emotional expression gets shut down early on. That bottling up of unprocessed emotion causes them to channel that energy into the only emotion that is socially acceptable for men: anger. This disconnection and tension in a man's relationships and inside himself expresses in external violence against others (oftentimes, women) and/or internal violence against himself, that shows up as addictions and other self-destructive behaviors.

The culture sets him up for a false hero's journey—a

quest for external means to fulfill him, from a career to a family to a sports car. He winds up in the proverbial midlife crisis, realizing he's done it all, but he's still not fulfilled, and he has no idea where to go.

Men, like women, are taught by patriarchal culture never to fully express their authentic selves. For further reading, an excellent book by Lewis Howes, *The Mask of Masculinity*, is a powerful expose on men's cultural conditioning. Howes explains how these defenses manifest for men and keep them from living their full lives, at the cost of their relationships, their happiness, and health.

COMMUNICATION BREAKDOWN

When men and women attempt to connect from our respective survival modes, our clay creates blocks in our communication. We argue or stonewall. We refuse affection. We engage in addictive behaviors to isolate and numb. We binge watch YouTube videos late into the night while our partner is sleeping. When we're in the same room, we turn to social media on our phones instead of connecting with each other.

All of these behaviors keep us out of our vulnerability and openness. It just doesn't feel safe to go there alone. Let alone together.

Many couples are stuck in this prison for years or decades. It feels normal. Perhaps the most painful aspect of this disconnection—which I lived through myself—is that when we're badly hurting, we don't allow ourselves to know we're hurting. The defenses are so strong that all the prison guards tell us is, *what else do you want? You have a good marriage. At least you're not single. He's a good man and a good dad.*

The guards work day and night to make everything seem okay.

The bar for what passes for a "perfectly fine" relationship in the patriarchy is set painfully low. Our culture has normalized the story that "passion doesn't last"—a prison guard in the cultural invisible inner prison. This story becomes a self-fulfilling prophecy, giving rise to evidence that gets captured by studies confirming and reinforcing it. In the cultural psyche, the prison security system functions a lot like it does in our individual subconscious. It's set up to protect, defend, and maintain the patriarchal status quo at all costs.

Because we don't talk about what goes on in our relationships, we don't realize that most couples carry the same secrets. Behind closed doors, there's so much loneliness, pain of disconnection, lack of sex drive and satisfaction, and addictions to whatever helps people cope with this pain of the failed promise of the "happily ever after."

PHYSICAL CONNECTION

Among the secrets that I hear from so very many couples

is that their sex lives dried up long ago. They live like roommates that have infrequent sex that they don't fully enjoy. They hide deep this painful secret, shrouded in shame, feeling like something's wrong with them and their relationship. In fact, they're in good company. *Newsweek* estimates that 15 to 20 percent of marriages are sexless—defined as having sex ten or fewer times a year.[29] Why are these couples not having sex?

A silent killer of sexual bliss in relationships is unprocessed trauma. Intergenerational, cultural, and personal layers of it.

For starters, the intergenerational trauma of patriarchal and religious conditioning is lodged in our subconscious. As a result of it, many men wrestle with the Madonna-whore complex, where subconsciously they can only relate to a woman either as a pure "virgin" wife and mother or a sexual being who they can allow themselves to get turned on by. Many women also struggle with integrating their sexuality that has historically been condemned as "sinful," establishing their sovereignty in the body that for millennia didn't belong to them, and being in touch with their desire, which has always been forbidden. This patriarchal denial of a woman's wholeness has deeply traumatized men, women, and relationships.

The cultural trauma continues to be perpetrated and triggered by the war on women—which military

---

29   Kathleen Deveny, "We're Not in the Mood," *Newsweek*, June 29, 2003.

operations are constantly evolving. Many "personal development," beauty, and fitness products and programs are infused by patriarchal propaganda and market to women's self-hate, shame, and guilt under the guise of empowerment. *You'll be empowered and unstoppable in the boardroom when you lose these pounds. Our product will make you look better, and when you look better, you'll feel more confident.* Our culture traps women in the hamster wheel, chasing surrogate confidence and empowerment, and feeling like failures when they just can't get there—a trend that many an industry capitalizes on. The tools of patriarchal oppression have become more sophisticated, subtle, insidious, and toxic as ever.

The accepted cultural entitlement to body judgment is a powerful weapon, and it's inescapable and omnipresent. Women's bodies are routinely scrutinized and policed in both the mainstream and social media. We internalize these judgments very early on in our childhood and carry on this war on our bodies within. As a result, it's really hard for a woman to have a loving and friendly relationship with her body. The trauma of cultural policing that gives out conditional approval based on conforming to rigid and often unachievable standards affects men too. The resulting self-hate and shame get masked by adaptations that disconnect people from their bodies and from each other, creating impenetrable barriers to true intimacy.

Likewise, there's no shortage of personal trauma that

walls off people's access to their desires, sexual expression, and satisfaction. This trauma doesn't have to be sexual in nature. Many traumatic experiences—feeling unsafe in our fullest authentic expression—have formed the protective barriers that inhibit our ability to deeply connect with ourselves and others. The depth and richness of our sex life is dependent on the depth and richness of our embodied connection. How turned on we are and how attracted we are to our partner is dependent on how emotionally safe we feel. The same trauma adaptations that are keeping us safe by blocking our access to vulnerability and prohibiting us from getting emotionally naked with our partner also block our access to authentic arousal and sexual bliss.

This vulnerability comes from a true place of safety, not a "fake it 'til you make it" strategy. That's why working on communication and behavior changes in your relationship—without addressing the traumas that these defenses are protecting—is like rearranging the deck chairs on the Titanic. No matter how much "progress" you make, your relationship is still on the collision course with the iceberg of unprocessed trauma.

Most of my clients have worked on their relationship before in therapy, coaching, or personal development programs. Many reached out to me feeling that something is very wrong with them and their relationship, because they had invested in all this work before, and they were still struggling. The first thing I tell my couples, is that it was not their failure—but that of the tools and approaches. And, of course, that what they're struggling with is not something that's wrong with them or their relationship in the first place. I love seeing people exhale, sit taller, and look lighter the moment they hear my explanation that the struggles they have been experiencing in their relationship are but defenses borne out of the intergenerational, cultural, and personal traumas that they both have—and not their fault, failure, or shortcoming.

As they begin their jailbreak journey of healing the traumas that these defenses are protecting, they become more and more connected with themselves, confident and comfortable in their own skin, and able to show up more fully and vulnerably with their partner. Their sexual magnetism amplifies as the clay comes off the gold and their beauty, their true colors shine through unobstructed by trauma defenses. Their ability to perceive the authentic beauty of their partner and be turned on by them grows exponentially, as the channels of their capacity for connection are cleared of the debris of old emotional wounds.

A pivotal moment of transformation happens when both people in a couple can be emotionally naked together while feeling safe and connected. This is where couples begin to break out together.

PARENTING IN PATRIARCHY

The patriarchal war on women doesn't spare motherhood. One of the biggest sources of pain for women is feeling like we are not good mothers. It's one thing to feel you're not reaching your full potential in your work in the world, that your romantic relationship is lacking intimacy, or that there's more hate than love in your relationship with yourself. But when you feel like you are failing as a mother—in all the little ways you want to be better for your children—this kind of pain cuts the deepest.

If only I make all his meals from scratch. If only I take her to all the playdates she wants to have. If only I never raise my voice, am never tired, annoyed, unavailable, cranky...then I will be okay.

Making women feel that they're not okay is like shooting fish in a barrel. A woman's core wound of being worth *less* carries its devastating effects into how she feels about herself as a mother. We want so badly not to perpetrate the same traumatic experiences we had in our childhoods, and we research how to bring our very best to motherhood. We read parenting books and immerse ourselves in different childrearing philosophies, and we try not to do and say the things our parents said and did.

But our children are the perfect mirrors of our unprocessed traumas. Every step of the way, they trigger the traumatic experiences of our own childhoods. When we're aware of it and have the toolset of working with what comes up, this becomes a golden opportunity, a perfect portal into healing. When we lack in awareness or skill, this creates a lot of suffering for us and for our kids.

The frustrating, painful experiences we carry in our subconscious have given rise to the prison guard of the inner critic, and that self-berating talk spills out into our parenting. We spend so much energy and effort to override our defenses: to always be present and not check out into social media or a glass of wine or an online shopping cart, to never lose it or explode in anger, to not criticize or say things that undercut our children in any way.

Perhaps you have a perfect day where you earn all the chips you possibly can making healthy meals from scratch and doing arts and crafts with your child; you're nurturing, emotionally available, and supportive in your energy, words, and actions.

At the end of the day, something triggers you, your capacity is overloaded, you snap, and there go the hard-won chips of your conditional worth as a mother. The house always wins.

As a mom, I'm very familiar with this cycle.

As long as our feeling good about ourselves as parents is conditional, we will always feel like we're failing. And the guilt. Its pain makes us disengage or get even more irritable, and to manage that, we disappear into work or Netflix. The guilt piles up ever higher.

The cycle feeds back into our trauma. It's rooted in the wound of worth-*less*-ness. It runs on a loop of confirmation of the worldview according to this wound—a distorted view of the world and ourselves through the walls of the invisible inner prison, through the layers of trauma. This worldview requires evidence to support its existence. Every "failure," "not enough," or "too much" serves as evidence reinforcing the prison walls.

As long as we're in this prison, we'll never ever feel good enough. Notwithstanding therapy, self-help books, personal growth seminars, expensive beauty regiments, punishing workouts, working on our marriages, and receiving promotions, bonuses, and awards.

There is a better way, which happens to be the easier and more joyful way: Take away the conditions of the approval of you. And instead, approve of yourself all the time. Instead of the unwinnable game, life becomes a game where you cannot fail.

As in, take all the chips back from the house of patriarchy and laugh all the way to the bank.

Take that in for a moment.

What would it be like to play a game where you cannot fail? Remember how we played when we were toddlers? Before we knew there was winning or losing in a game, we played for the sake of playing. We made a tower of blocks, it fell down, and we rebuilt it without blinking an eye. We made something even better.

We did not play to win. We didn't know we could lose.

This is the game I invite you to experience right now.

It begins with being honest, open, and vulnerable with yourself about your own feelings, emotions, needs, and desires. We have long, traumatic histories of not being seen and heard and not having our needs met. So seeing, hearing, and meeting your own needs—and modeling this for your children—is healing and revolutionary.

As you progress on your jailbreak journey, you learn to recognize, interrogate, and strip away the conditions of your acceptance. When you are okay unconditionally, it changes everything. Then you can be unconditionally okay with your children. They see and feel your unconditional acceptance, and they feel they have the space to be unconditionally okay. When the inner critic gets quiet, you no longer have the urge to be critical of others— whether out loud or in your mind.

Until we make this internal shift of being unconditionally okay within ourselves, we will never allow our children to be unconditionally okay. No matter how many parenting books we read. Just like our parents could not allow us to be unconditionally okay, because they didn't have that internal permission. For them, too, as we were growing up, we were triggering the unprocessed traumas from their childhoods, which they likely had little or no awareness of or tools to work with. Same was true for their dynamic with their parents, and so on.

When we're driven by PSD to keep trying harder, doing more, or being something different than we already are, we bring this subconscious programming into our parenting. It comes through in our energy, our tone of voice, what we say and do, and the way we model not being comfortable in our own skin, a lack of approval of ourselves.

This is what will imprint on our children.

Now that you have the awareness of what happens when traumas get triggered, and what's involved in the healing journey, I hope that you can feel more compassion for yourself on this parenting adventure—as well as for that of your parents—as adults with unprocessed childhood traumas and as children who experienced and inherited them through no fault of their own.

When we get on our jailbreak journey, we heal not only ourselves—we break the cycle of imprisonment for generations.

We claim the gift of unconditional self-approval and pass it along. We are now able to be unconditionally approving of our children, and they can learn to approve of themselves.

The joyful, amazing thing about this process is that when you break the cycle, you get instant feedback. You see that joy, freedom, and ease reflected in your children. This reinforcement of your own parenting is in turn hugely healing for your inner child.

Learn to recognize when you're playing the old game. Notice when you are making your self-acceptance conditional. Pour some good medicine of self-compassion on this wound. Remember, you're shifting out of the inter-generational, trauma-rooted, unwinnable prison game of *how much can I bear?* to the one where you always win, the game of *how good can it get?*

Notice when the prison guards perk up and throw evidence at you of why this is not possible and would never work. Smile at them. Thank them for looking out for you.

Use the Re-Power Tool to interrupt the trauma hijack and get back in your body and your sovereignty.

Then get back to what you desire. What's the next step in the game of *how good can it get?* What can you do or stop doing right now to elevate your experience? Stand up, stretch, dance, smile, breathe, have a glass of water, share a nice belly laugh with your little one. Or put on some music that matches your mood and allow yourself to express the anger or sadness you're feeling, through your body, through movement and voice.

Have your children join you in this game. The younger they are, the better they know how to play it. They haven't unlearned it yet. They can teach us a lot.

THE VALUE OF EMOTIONS

It can be terrifying as a mother to commit to bringing your authentic, whole self into parenting. With our full emotional expressions comes the expression of emotions that we were told were not okay. As we feel these emotions in front of our children, we may hesitate around expressing them, and opt to suppress them instead.

We were taught that we must always be nurturing and

positive, and never angry or sad. Our culture has labeled these emotions as "negative," and told us that "negative" emotions are not allowed. Self-help and personal development industries perpetuate this harmful cultural conditioning by promoting positivity. This approach is shortsighted and dangerous. It drives our natural emotions, artificially labeled as "negative," deeper into shadow, wraps them in shame and stuffs them into our subconscious, growing the underwater part of the iceberg that we hit sooner or later. Since we don't see it coming, the collision and its consequences can be devastating. Explosive outbursts at work and at home, isolation, self-hate, anxiety, depression, and addictions are but a few common expressions of the drowned emotions. There's increasing awareness of the mind-body connection and the role of unprocessed emotions in undesirable health expressions—from headaches and backaches to hormonal and immune system issues.

As we know from the jailbreak process, it is only by fully expressing these emotions that we can discharge them and move them out of our bodies. When we don't, they can metastasize into health conditions, a lack of intimacy and connection in our relationships, and a cap on our genius in our work.

By suppressing these emotions in ourselves, we model suppression to our children.

Healing PSD means healing the illusory divide that labels emotions as "positive" or "negative." Emotions are energy in motion. They are meant to move through the body to be expressed and discharged. We run into trouble when our suppressed emotions hijack us, either because we didn't learn healthy, appropriate emotional expressions, or because we were denied the space to feel okay with them. That's why we fear our emotions. We're scared that if we give ourselves the permission to get in touch with them, we will explode, we'll be overwhelmed, and the people around us will judge and reject us.

With practice, you develop an awareness of the difference between your prison guards and your true, authentic self. You can notice when the prison guards show up as thoughts that make you feel contracted and defensive, as opposed to expansive, relaxed, and connected. You can greet these guards, thank them for their service, and then you can speak to feeling this way. To your child, you can say, "Honey, I'm feeling sad right now. I'm feeling angry." You can reassure them it is not about them or anything they're doing wrong, but that you're aware of your own feelings. This will help them develop empathy for others and also for themselves. This will teach them that they are okay no matter how they feel inside. That they're accepted and loved, unconditionally. That they don't need to be ashamed and hide how they truly feel.

You can then model jailbreak for them: Allow yourself to express that feeling. If you're feeling sad, you can allow the tears to come, allow yourself to make sad sounds, and move that emotion through your body. You can put on sad music and move to the sad music together. You can start a conversation about sadness, ask them whether there is any part of them that is feeling sad, and honor and invite that part out to play.

End this practice by creating embodied physical comfort. Hug each other, breathe with each other, look into each other's eyes, and shift into pleasure mindfulness together. When I practice this with my daughter, I find that the expression of anger, sadness, or fear, followed by the experience of comfort, inevitably leads to smiles, giggles, and explosive laughter. This practice allows us to connect so much deeper than we ever could in bypassing the authentic emotion and jumping right into fake "positivity." Counterintuitively, when we go fully into a challenging emotion, we always and organically end on a high note. It's an inevitable outcome of creating loving and accepting space for our true, authentic experience—for our whole selves. When we do it, we send the message to our child: *You're loved and accepted, always. Every part of you. No part of you is unwanted or bad. All of you is precious.* This is a powerful message that they'll imprint for life. We can only send it through experience—words alone won't cut it.

These practices are basic emotional hygiene—like brushing and flossing our teeth—that should be taught to every human early on. Our children pick up on our stifled emotions. They know when we're not allowing ourselves to express our full authentic selves. They can feel it. And when they take our lead and don't express themselves, they begin to keep secrets from us and even from themselves.

The Disney/Pixar movie *Inside Out* is a brilliant introduction to this topic. In the movie, each of the basic emotions is represented by a character living inside a young girl, Riley. She was going through a move and was devastated from losing her friends, her home, and her hockey team, and she was anxious at the prospect of a new city and a new school. One of the themes of the movie is that the character of Joy believed that to save the day, she alone would need to make Riley feel good again. In the course of the adventures these characters go through, Joy realizes she cannot do her job without Sadness.

We can develop the skillset to access our emotions safely. And we can teach these skills to our children.

THRIVING IN SADNESS

I faced a similar challenge a few years ago when our family was breaking up. I was separating from my daughter's dad, and we were moving away from the house where she grew up. My daughter was leaving her school and her friends.

I was focused on survival. I packed up our things, put our house on the market, got rid of stuff, and took care of the logistics. What I was modeling for my daughter was this "suck it up" attitude, just getting from point A to point B. I wasn't expressing my grief or my anger. I was being "a strong woman" who gets the job done. I was suppressing my emotions. I did not want to alarm my daughter or bring her down.

At the time, I did not realize there was anything wrong with that. I saw that my daughter was just…happy. She was cheerful. Happy-go-lucky all the time.

And then, as tends to happen, those more difficult, challenging emotions began leaking out in small things.

She would have major meltdowns about minor things, like not being able to have the dessert she wanted. Or she would become upset about things that were seemingly unrelated to what was going on in the moment. At the same time, I was facing my own challenging, unprocessed emotions. I was grieving the end of our family as we knew it. We were selling the house that we loved, the house in which we had welcomed our daughter, and that we had thought we would live in for the rest of our lives.

When I finally allowed myself to start grieving, and I began expressing my sadness and talking about it with my daughter, she was reluctant to come meet me there.

"Mommy, why would I want to feel sad?" She said. "It's not a good feeling."

I realized the example I had set. I had reinforced the societal conditioning by communicating to her that being positive was desirable and feeling sad was not okay. Sadness had become a dangerous place where one would never want to go.

We watched *Inside Out* together and began to have conversations about the value of sadness. I put on a sad song that we could move together to: "Your True Colors," from the movie *Trolls*. As Justin Timberlake sang—*you with the sad eyes, don't get discouraged*—I let tears come and expressed what I was feeling sad about. Little by little, she joined me in showing the true colors of the feelings that were present for her.

Expressing our emotions together has created more points of connection for us. It was so valuable, particularly at this time of a big life transition. It has brought us closer together.

Before expressing our full range of feelings, we only had one point of connection: our positivity and humor. The myriad of other emotional expressions was offline. When we plugged in and connected to all these centers of emotion, the intimacy of our connection multiplied. She started to share things with me that she had not been forthcoming about before. Because now, all of it was okay. All of it was welcomed as precious.

This shift toward realness, vulnerability, connection, and intimacy has started a new era in our relationship. I'm grateful that we have been able to connect deeply now, and we both experience the value of cultivating this connection as we move toward her teenage years.

Before the call to show up authentically for my daughter, I had been operating from within a shell of defenses. I was operating as a "strong woman" while shutting out all the vulnerable parts of myself. As I reclaimed those pieces of myself, it allowed us to create space for her to own all her vulnerabilities, too.

MINING THE GOLD FROM OUR PARENTS

Throughout this experience of connecting with my daughter, I developed a deeper understanding and compassion for my parents, who had not been consistently emotionally available as I was growing up. In my childhood, PSD expressed in anger, detachment, and drinking for dad. It drove my mom's anxiety, depression, and passive aggression. In my adulthood, I had spent over twenty years collecting and honing the tools of trauma resolution. These were tools my parents never had access to in their own lives. They grew up in the PSD prison and had no reference points outside of it. They had no opportunity or awareness of what could be different and what could be healed.

For years we had been locked in intense, bitter arguments. Our defenses were constantly up, and we were always ready to fire our weapons at one another. We related only clay to clay. We needed to get to the gold underneath.

After years of playing out trauma patterns, I was on my jailbreak journey, consciously creating my life. I had much happiness and joy that I desired to share with them.

I craved connection with my parents in a whole new, conscious, post-jailbreak way—not through the game of *how much can I bear?* but through the game of *how good can it get?*

They were not available for that. They weren't able to hear me or relate to my experiences. We weren't able to connect. When freedom vibes made it through the prison bars, they registered as foreign and threatening. Their survival attunement didn't resonate with the melody of thriving.

Whenever I would show up in my joy, they would try to pull me into anxiety. Upon registering happiness, they would instantly pivot the conversation to something to worry about.

Me: "We're going to Hawaii! We'll be staying at the black sand beach!"

Mom: "Did you know, black sand will ruin your bathing suits. It doesn't wash out."

Me: "I just signed the biggest contract in my business to date!"

Dad: "You may end up in a higher tax bracket. Are you saving enough money to pay your taxes?"

Did you remember to worry about this, and this, and this?

Initially in our conversations, I would get triggered. Pleasure police would pull me over: *did you know you were driving over the pleasure speed limit?* I would get pulled into the clay of my own anger and disconnection.

Are you not hearing me? Are you not seeing me? My plea-sure, my joy? You never understand me! I wanted so badly to have them appreciate huge quantum leaps in my life. Not the ones from the degrees I'd gotten and the professional accomplishments I'd accrued, but from how far I had come in my inner life. Not the house and the business, but the true wealth that I'd built on the interior of my being. The jailbreak that had freed me from the imprisonment of anxiety, depression, fears, scarcity, and self-hate—that I once was certain was a life sentence. The inner shifts that opened the portals and gave me access to the luxury of experiences I'd never imagined or thought possible— deep intimacy, connection, love, excitement, happiness, joy—not as fleeting, flash-in-the-pan, momentary flukes, but as my new, stable baseline, my new normal, in the new game of *how good can it get?*

But on this one particular phone call, when I told my dad what I was celebrating and he didn't share in my joy, I finally realized: he *couldn't* share my excitement. This kind of joy was so outside of my parents' experience that they could not go there with me.

I did not say, "You never understand me."

Instead, I said, "Dad, it means so much for me to be able to share my wins with you. I want so much for you to be able to feel my joy and celebrate with me. It makes me so sad when we just bypass that and move on to the next agenda item. I understand that it's hard not to be anxious and wait for the other shoe to drop. I understand the pull of that pattern you had to develop to survive. But I need you to celebrate with me."

To my great surprise, my dad's tone changed. "I really want to," he said, "but I don't think I can. You have to understand, there's has been not much room for enjoyment or celebration in our lives. I think it's too late for us to change."

"It's okay, Dad," I said. "We can start by taking baby steps. Let's just take a few moments to feel good about what I just shared with you."

"Okay, let's do that," he said. It was one of our deepest moments of connection.

I never felt emotionally safe growing up because of his volatility and anger. I was always hypervigilant around him. My defenses would trigger his defenses, which would re-trigger mine. These interactions layered so much grief, frustration, and anger—layers of clay—over our connection. But at last, we came together gold to gold.

As I showed up more authentically in my relationship with my parents, these moments of connection became possible, and more frequent. They became a reference point for finding the gold. I was amazed at their willingness to meet me there. It turned out it wasn't too late for them after all to start learning the new game of *how good can it get?*

Jailbreak is contagious. Once you've accumulated a reservoir of joy and pleasure and gained access to greater freedom and authenticity, you become the center of a vortex that draws in others around you and transforms their experiences and your relationships. This is the "how to" of being the change you want to see in the world.

A SISTERHOOD OF JAILBREAKERS

Our prison guards, as you now know, are in the business of sustaining the status quo. They have been reading this book with you and may have been taking every opportunity to poke at the content and raise objections. When you put down the book, to make sure you don't follow through with your jailbreak, they're likely to employ what I call *the fog of forgetfulness*. I predict that it will erase 90 percent of everything you just took in, and other parts of the prison security system—procrastination, distractions, and stories about how this will never work for you and is not worth the investment of your time and energy—will pick up the slack. The prison security system is very sophisticated. Now that the invisible inner prison has been made visible, the prison guards are going to make sure to discredit or erase that information from your consciousness and arrest your motivation for jailbreak.

What I've found in my own jailbreak experience and those of my clients, is that the mainstream culture retraumatizes us and reinforces the status quo of the prison security system all day long. Thus, crucial to the success of the journey is support from a counter-cultural community of jailbreakers. If the jailbreak system and the tools

I've shared in this book spoke to you, I hope you put them to good use immediately. You can certainly make a lot of progress if you apply them and make them an integral part of your life. But if you experience resistance and slow or little progress working on your jailbreak by yourself, it's not a sign that there's something wrong with you or with the system. It's just that our culture reinforces the status quo 24/7. That's why it's really hard to jailbreak in isolation.

I initially formed a community of jailbreakers because I needed it for myself. I knew that without the support of this circle of people who were conscious creators of their lives, the resistance from my prison guards would make the jailbreak journey feel like pushing a boulder up the hill. Sisyphus' labor belongs in the old prison game of *how much can I bear?* In the new game of *how good can it get?* I wanted the journey to be easy and fun. Creating a supportive community was essential for that.

It is an uphill battle to break out of our cultural and ancestral conditioning and trauma. When we have community, we gather collective energy and guidance for our journey. Our fellow jailbreakers can point out exactly where we're stepping into the traps the prison guards have set out for us. They help fuel our motivation when it's running low, celebrate our wins with us, and offer support to get through the challenges. They hold the mirrors to help us appreciate our courageous journey with a compassionate and friendly gaze.

Another gift of the jailbreakers' community is opportunities for shadow work. Whenever a jailbreaker shares her experience, the parts of others hidden in shadow—light or dark—get triggered to let us know they're there, ready to be seen, healed, reclaimed, and integrated. The parts that have been forced into exile into the subconscious by trauma—as too bright, too much, not okay—feel safe to show up and be reclaimed and reintegrated, embraced and welcomed by a supportive community. Everyone's preciousness is reflected back by everyone else. Vulnerability, anger, sadness, joy, jealousy, celebration, bliss, or confusion—all these disowned, forbidden, and shamed parts of ourselves experience acceptance. Often, for the first time in our lives. This happens both in our virtual community and at jailbreak retreats, turbocharging the journey for everyone, moving us all to freedom faster.

High tide lifts all boats. When we make a discovery within ourselves and share it, we help others see the invisible and do the impossible too. By showing up and sharing from our own journey, we give others permission to go further.

All our traumas were received in a community. That's why need a community to heal them. In the words of a client,

> *I grew up with people reflecting distorted versions of myself. What I learned from them about myself was all wrong. You*

see and reflect my True Person. This is what I've been needing to heal all these years. This has been invaluable for me.

When we share our experiences, shared pain becomes lighter, shared joy becomes amplified, and a shared journey becomes an exciting adventure. I'm so grateful to be on this adventure with my fellow jailbreakers. I live for my clients' jailbreak moments, and I'm privileged to witness them every day. Recently, a client shared this moment with me:

I realized that I can be friends with myself and actually support myself. I had thought I was supposed to push myself, fight with myself, and every day I would wake up with anxiety. I would wake up with a jolt and jump into the battlefield to accomplish what I had to accomplish. Now, I can be a friend to myself. I can be a friend to my body.

We can shift from playing the prison game of proving ourselves to playing the game where nothing we do or don't do ever adds to or subtracts from our worth—because our worth is absolute and unconditional and doesn't require proof. Then we may set goals and accomplish them because they give us pleasure. We may choose to enhance our beauty with makeup and dress because it gives us pleasure, not to mask our "imperfections" and make ourselves acceptable to society. We feel safe, free, and excited to show as our whole, shiny, authentic selves as human beings, partners, and parents.

If this resonates with you, we would love to welcome you in the jailbreakers' community. Find out how to join us on my website. Your presence will lift us all higher.

CREATION AND DESTRUCTION

As you go through your jailbreak, you will experience turbulence in your interactions with others. You're going to ask for more from every area of your life, including your relationships. You're going to ask the people around you to show up in more authentic ways, and in ways that better support you.

Each relationship will be redefined and recalibrated. Some relationships will not survive this recalibration. Some people will not want to go to the next level with you.

It's important to make space to grieve, to let go, and to welcome new and deeper connections. It's an ancient principle that creation and destruction go hand in hand. We can't always create something new on old foundations. Some of the people around you will be inspired to dismantle the old and create something new within themselves. Others will not.

Settling for the safety of the status quo is a popular choice in our culture. The path of creation lies outside of the safety perimeter. At twenty-two I left my home in Russia for New York City, letting go of my old life before I knew what the new one would look like. I came to New York for what I thought would be a two-week trip, which stretched to almost twenty years. In that time, I earned two graduate degrees in psychology, served hundreds of people and businesses, got married, had a wonderful daughter, made amazing friends, and had great adventures.

Again, I let go of the safety of my old life when I chose to leave my marriage. I knew it was not going to be a popular decision, and I agonized over it for a long time. Years of running in the hamster wheel of "working on our marriage" had drained me not only of knowing who I was—but of the memory of that feeling. Resentment became my dominant emotion. I was a dead woman walking. We all deserved better than that. I craved to feel fully alive, vibrant, and happy. I wanted to be that kind of a mother for our daughter. I felt it was my responsibility to become that person for her and for me. I was forty years old, and about to become a single mom. I said "no" to my old life without knowing what I was saying "yes" to.

It turned out that "no" opened up the gates to the "yes," and exponentially improved the game of *how good can it get?* in my life and work. Our daughter is thriving. She cherishes her relationship with her dad, and her life is greatly enriched by other deep and meaningful relationships that I've been able to create since I came back to life.

Every big "yes" begins with a big "no."

Taking the leap to destroy the old before the creation of the new feels so unsafe. It's a free fall. It triggers all of our old survival instincts and brings our old traumas to the surface. Jailbreak is not for the faint of heart, and it is not a journey to be taken alone.

You'll need a support network that will see you, validate, and support you. Gather the people who will invest in you and uphold and celebrate the person you are becoming before you even know who she is. When you're in the ruins of the old, you need people who will not judge you, people you won't be "too much" for, people who'll have your back.

Not everyone will be up for this transformation. People in our lives tend to nail us on the cross of our old identity. When we're trying to break out of jail, that's the last thing we need. You need to surround yourself with people who are committed to your highest good—even if they don't understand it—over sustaining the status quo, courageous souls who are excited to welcome—and even midwife—the new and evolving you into the world.

The best thing you can do to attract these people is show up in your gold. Some people will resonate with your authentic shine, and they will draw close to it. Some people will find their old traumas are triggered, and they will cover up with clay.

Nourish your heart with compassion. Create space to grieve losses in this process. Even the most positive and desirable of changes involve loss of the old. Even the most painful past deserves and needs to be properly grieved. Make space for these emotions to move through your body. Trust that this recalibration—however intense the turbulence—will open up space for something even better than you can imagine at this time, a whole new level of depth in your existing relationships and a whole other caliber of new people that you will attract into your life. These transformed and new relationships will have something in common—they'll uphold, celebrate, and amplify your gold, all parts of the whole and authentic you.

In a community of people who connect with you gold to gold, you'll find a whole new level of support, love, and celebration of your genius that you likely have not experienced before. There's no reference for it in the invisible inner prison. There, it doesn't exist.

I realized in cultivating my own jailbreak that it was essential to surround myself with fellow jailbreakers. Some are coaches, trainers, and healers I have reached out to because I want them in my life as guides. I also find that the more clay comes off my gold, the more I attract people who show up in their authentic beauty and power. We recognize, reflect, and amplify that in each other, and we grow together.

I want this for you.

I want the world to experience your gold. I want to experience your true beauty and power. If there's anything I can do to support your jailbreak journey, please let me know. You can connect with me at www.drvalerie.com where you can contact me directly and find additional tools and resources for your jailbreak.

CHAPTER SEVEN

SUCCESS ON THE OUTSIDE

If you look at what this country accomplished only using half of its talent, just think of the potential for the future...we, by some rather stupid decisions, essentially put half of our talent on the sidelines.

—WARREN BUFFETT

WOMEN OFTEN FIND MY WORK EITHER BECAUSE they are orchestrating jailbreak in their personal life or because they're working to harness their genius in their professional success. Interestingly, whatever string we start pulling on tends to unwind the other track as well.

You already heard the story of Jessica, who, in chapter 5, was dating all the wrong guys. Until her jailbreak, she didn't see what was driving this attraction, or the choices she had available to her in her dating life. The same was true in her career.

Jess felt miserable and stuck in her job. She was productive, creative, and a high performer whose results outpaced the others on her team. She was frustrated that management was not recognizing her talents and promoting her. Worse, they were asking her to work longer hours, but had not offered more pay.

In her mind, at the time, she saw this as a "perfect job." It had more pros than cons: She had a short commute, and enough flexibility to make it to the gym after hours. She enjoyed a few of her coworkers, though she also noticed that those relationships were tinged with a lack of reciprocity. She often helped her colleagues with projects and contributed to their success, but she didn't receive the same help from them. Just like in her personal life, she was over-giving and under-receiving. She was emotionally and financially spent.

Of course, Jess had a choice: she could leave the company. But her prison guards told her stories that connected to her desire for safety and her fear of failure. *Appreciate your commute and your coworkers. You don't know how good you have it. What if you're not all that talented? If you go to a different company, they'll see right through you. You'll lose it all.*

As always, the prison guards took us right to the places she needed to heal. We explored her relationship with her parents, who hadn't truly seen her and nurtured her. Growing up, she'd felt like the black sheep of the family. She didn't know what she was doing; she was not good enough; she was so sickly and fragile and incapable of surviving on her own. All of these wounds, you can imagine, were keeping her locked in a job that was draining her, alongside a string of relationships that were doing the same.

As we unwound and healed these traumas, Jess began to feel more confident and comfortable in her own skin. The story in her mind began to change. She no longer told herself, *I can never leave this job, it's too secure and convenient.* Now, she realized, *I must get the hell out of here. It's killing me.*

Within a few weeks, she left her toxic job for a different company, where her new position gave her a lot of creative freedom right away. Her manager raved about her. She felt valued, seen, and appreciated. Her new position mirrored her new relationship with herself. She was quickly promoted. Even better, she traded her "good enough" commute for the freedom to work remotely. She got to travel more and took "work-cations" around the world while still making a good living and enjoying herself.

This job, which had appeared so quickly once she'd opened her mind to it, had not seemed possible to her before her jailbreak. When our minds are protected and surrounded by the prison guards, we cannot imagine what a better life may look and feel like.

It takes courage to begin the jailbreak journey. Sometimes it takes pain. On that path is a moment where you realize, *I don't have to suffer anymore.* That is the moment in which you step into leadership within your own life. You can use the same jailbreak process to step into leadership in your relationships, in your professional field, and within your organization.

It begins with questioning the status quo.

LEADERS QUESTION EVERYTHING

Whether you're looking to transform your individual career or your organization, professional jailbreak begins with status-quo-disruptive questions, such as:

What are you avoiding? or *What are you tolerating?*

These questions can be broken down in innumerable ways. Where is your company's vision playing it safe? What gets in the way of your creative thinking? What products or services or tasks are holding you back from your true potential?

The organizational structures and processes that keep your company safe—and limited—can point you to the trauma adaptations of your company, or even your field.

There is a scene in the movie *Ocean's 12* in which a thief is planning to steal a Fabergé egg from a museum. The thief has carefully planned his heist, and he arrives in the dark hall after hours to see a web of lasers tracing randomly across the floor. He's done his research. This is the museum's sophisticated security system, and if he makes a false step across the hall, the alarms will be triggered, and his entire plan will be foiled. He begins a carefully rehearsed dance, diving under and hopping over the laser beams until he gets to the jewels.

Jailbreaking within an organization is like that.

Sophisticated security structures are built into your company—or your career—to keep it safe. Some of these structures may be relics of the status quo. You can recognize this when the prison guards declare: *Everybody is doing business this way. Everybody is doing sales this way. Everybody is doing marketing this way.*

But is "this way" holding you back from an exponential breakthrough?

JAILBREAKING A BUSINESS

Trauma conditions us to play it safe instead of tapping into our creativity. When I began applying what I knew about trauma to my business, I began to see where the status quo was creating limitations in my company. I was making all the decisions in my business, and yet I was doing things in ways that were not bringing me pleasure because everyone in my industry was doing the same things the same way. I was not questioning it; I was playing it safe. I was not operating in my zone of genius.

The symptoms of these limitations were clear. I was stressed. I'd hit a revenue plateau. I was working so hard, and yet my work was not bringing me joy, pleasure, or the financial results I desired. I knew I could get better results for my clients faster, but I was not thinking outside the box for how to accomplish that. I was not even aware there was a box.

Once I realized that my own trauma patterns were playing out in how I had set up and was running my business, that they formed the walls of the invisible inner prison—I saw that I could apply the jailbreak process to bring more happiness and fulfillment to my company.

This realization, followed by analysis of what intergenerational, cultural, and personal trauma patterns were at play, was step one of the jailbreak process: waking up in prison.

I then began asking, *What thoughts, (the mind), business structures (the body), behaviors, and choices (actions) are keeping my business "safe"?*

This is step two of the jailbreak system: getting to know the prison guards.

I asked myself, *What choices do you continue to make because you've had success with them in the past? What steps do you default to simply because everyone else in your industry is doing it this way?*

I wanted to reach a large number of people. I wanted more revenue, as well as time and location independence. These problems could not be solved within my current business model, which was a clinical psychology practice in an office in New York, where I saw one client at a time.

When I tried to brainstorm solutions from within the status quo, I only came up with more problems. Realistically, I thought, if I wanted to make more money in my current business model, I would need to hire more employees and bring on more trainees. Forget about location independence if I had more staff; I would have to be there to supervise them and make sure everything ran smoothly. If I wanted to make more money, I would need to put in more time. I'd end up creating more stress for myself. I was stuck thinking inside the box.

This is what everyone in my industry was doing. It was what I had learned in school about how to operate as a psychologist. To build a successful practice was the "happily ever after" in the industry. I'd gotten there—but my "happily ever after" wasn't all that happy.

Once the invisible walls of my business's inner prison became visible, I was able to look at these problems from the perspective of my true desires and my true genius. When I anchored into my desire to reach more people, I realized I could pour my over twenty years of exploration into a system that I could teach. I could teach people to become their own therapists, and their own healers, and I could train practitioners who would go on to reach more people in their work.

In this new structure, there was no ceiling on my revenue, nor on my time and location independence. My business could expand exponentially. With each stage of growth I encountered a new level of jailbreak that required me to meet new prison guards, inquire what they were protecting me from, and use that guidance to reach deeper levels of healing. Deeper healing would open up greater degrees of freedom, where I would be tasked with mastering new levels of the game of *how good can it get?*

To go higher in our work in the world, we need to go deeper in our inner work. Otherwise, we'd be building on a shaky foundation of unprocessed trauma, which like a time-bomb threatens to go off as self-sabotage, stress, illness, or relationships rupture any moment.

My discovery and transformation created more freedom, more abundance, more expansion, more visibility, and more power in my business. I asked myself what clients I desired to serve, what leaders, companies, and audiences I wanted to impact. I allowed my desire to lead me outside the prison walls. As a result, opportunities began opening up for me and my company that I wouldn't have dared to imagine prior to taking my business through the jailbreak process.

My clients' experiences have been confirming the game-changing impact of jailbreak on their businesses. As one business owner and CEO reflected:

Working with Dr. Valerie has honestly facilitated the biggest leap of my life! I was hooked from the first time I heard her message about high-performing women's missing link to happiness and it not being our fault. This message felt contrary to every "try harder" piece of advice I'd had all my life.

In only a few months I have stepped to a whole new level—my energy has shifted dramatically (and people are asking what's different about me). I don't have anxiety silently hanging around anymore, and I'm attracting opportunities and favor in my business at a whole new level I couldn't have dreamed of. People are now contacting me out of the blue, doors opening with ease, my ideal clients are flocking to me...whereas the last few years before, years of trauma, working hard, solo parenting, I was tired and it all felt such hard work. I feel I know who I am, with greater clarity than ever and the confidence to walk into the destiny that Dr. Valerie showed me in the mirror she constantly holds up to me.

MODELING SUCCESS

As I transformed my company, I began to recognize what I was modeling to my daughter. She saw that as I thought more creatively about my business, I brought more happiness, satisfaction, and fulfillment into our lives. I first thought of this modeling as a side benefit, and later realized this was another core desire that propelled my work: I want my daughter to grow up seeing and knowing she can create *anything*, and she doesn't need to suffer.

The game I grew up learning was to keep my head down and *work, work, work*. My mother, grandmother, and great-grandmother modeled it and passed it down. But my daughter witnesses my retreats, talks, and trainings, and she gets to experience work that centers on and generates joy and pleasure.

Already at eight years old, I know she won't have it any other way.

The evidence is mounting: even millennia-old patterns can be interrupted in just one generation. This is the true power of jailbreak. By doing this work, you're changing not only your own destiny, but that of generations to come.

ACKNOWLEDGING FEAR

The prison security system keeps your business operating in place. When you start to question the status quo and make changes, your prison guards will go on high alert. This is a reality you're going to face. They will tell convincing stories to keep you in your zone of safety.

I can't make all these changes. People depend on me. Not everyone will be on board with this. I'll lose clients. I'll lose revenue. I can't possibly afford to do that.

These stories are keeping you from your zone of genius.

By now, you're familiar with the voices of your prison guards. Jailbreaking your business happens in just the same way that jailbreak happens in your personal, internal process. You need to recognize the invisible walls of the status quo. You must meet the prison guards and get to know them well. Then you need to bribe them by creating embodied safety and following your pleasure.

In a business transformation, this process happens

internally at the level of the individual, and it also happens organization-wide. The living, breathing participants of your organizational change must be brought on board. The people in your organization have their own internal security systems that create fear and resistance in them.

We meet them where they are, and help them upgrade the internal security systems—from ones where the prison guards are keeping them stuck, to ones where the bodyguards are protecting them on their journey of change, growth, and expansion.

When I teach this system to teams and companies, I teach the same five-step system that every person can apply to their internal process. It enables people to feel safe—a necessary and so often completely overlooked condition for organizational change that actually works. When they feel safe, people come on board with their authentic genius, and they pour it into the vision.

Transformation happens holographically from there: internal change in each individual becomes change across the whole organization.

Resistance occurs when the prison guards speak up. We cannot simply push back against resistance. That tactic gets us nowhere. It causes people to shut down and disengage. When people are not feeling safe, morale drops, teamwork plummets, and absenteeism increases.

Instead, we acknowledge these defenses as voices of the security system that is keeping us safe. We use the same mind-body tools to create safety that enables people to engage in challenging conversations gold to gold versus clay to clay. These practices have the power to melt tension and transform conflict into collaboration.

FROM CONVERSATION TO ACTION

Anxiety and depression are signals that you're not living from a place of your authentic genius in your work or personal life. Symptoms appear on an organizational level when a company is not leveraging the genius of its people. A company can get depressed, as characterized by low energy and motivation, apathy, poor focus, and low self-esteem, sometimes even thoughts of suicide. A company can experience anxiety, marked by stress disproportionate to the impact of actual events, restlessness, racing thoughts, excessive worry that just wouldn't go away, and fear. Companies have addictions—reaching for the same coping strategies of poor management and suboptimal systems, seeking safety in the familiar, leaning on the status quo of "we've always done it this way," even though these strategies don't work—just like with other addictions, they mask but do not solve the underlying issues. Companies also face internal and external relationship problems.

Jessica's company lost her to a competitor because they didn't question the status quo of management practices, despite long-standing evidence of poor teamwork, low morale, lackluster performance, and employee dissatisfaction. When employees don't feel seen, heard, celebrated, or safe, they don't unfurl all their talents, they don't play full out.

Companies must create the conditions for the genius of their people to be recognized and nurtured.

If you find yourself in the kind of situation Jess was in, working in an environment that does not recognize your talents, communicate your needs and desires, and describe how they align with the company's needs and desires. Center your conversations around what is right and how we can make it better, rather than what is wrong and how it can be fixed. These conversations take the win-win philosophy up a notch. They avoid blame and thus minimize resistance from the defenses. They acknowledge and celebrate what works, inviting all to join in the game of *how good can it get?*

Once Jess created a sense of safety for herself, she was able to have these kinds of conversations with her management. The company's management was not open to the new game. While the conversations were friendly, Jessica didn't get much more than a patronizing pat on the head.

This kind of response is characteristic of the management structures in companies that are stuck playing the old game. Many companies attempt to create a friendly and inclusive environment for all their employees, but patriarchal conditioning often governs company policy and the behaviors of individuals—across the gender spectrum. There are many factors in a company's "subconscious," or blind spots, that create and sustain a toxic environment that drives out top diverse talent or hurts their advancement. For example, instead of hearing and seeing their employees' needs and perspectives, a company's management may be unconsciously reinforcing the patriarchal power differential based on gender, race, sexual orientation, and job title. Most companies do not explicitly set out to exercise the power differential, so they are genuinely surprised and even shocked when we begin to uncover unconscious practices that are in direct conflict with their vision and values and are eager to correct them.

More and more people are starting to take notice of toxic company cultures. Shareholders are beginning to hold organizations accountable for diversity, equity, and inclusion. Consumers and customers are becoming more conscious and discerning about doing business with companies whose values they feel aligned with.

The role of the psychologist is to help a client uncover how their subconscious drives their conscious thoughts, behaviors, and choices. As a consultant, I bring my psychologist skillset to teams and companies, to help them see how their subconscious beliefs and biases result in high turnover, low morale, absenteeism, presenteeism, interpersonal conflict, advancement and leadership challenges, and poor engagement with the company's mission. Each of these problems negatively affects people's mental—and sometimes physical—health and well-being, as well as the bottom line of the business.

SUBCONSCIOUS SABOTAGE

The subconscious beliefs and biases of a company often play themselves out in very subtle ways. I have had conversations with so many women who have been dismissed in meetings, who get less airtime than their male colleagues, or who are regularly asked to do work outside their direct responsibilities.

Michelle was one of these women. She led the board of a nonprofit that had been entrusted with a massive state-wide initiative. The rest of the board happened to be all older men. Whenever Michelle presented her ideas, they were very quick to shut her down and dismiss her.

As women, we're conditioned to turn to self-improvement to mend relational problems, and Michelle dove into books on how to improve communication. None of it was helping. Still the board shut down what she had to contribute.

One day a new board member, a younger man, who had awareness of the patriarchal status quo at play, saw the pattern: Michelle voiced her idea in a meeting, and she was immediately rejected.

This board member then took her idea, reworded it,

and presented the idea to the board as his own. He did not reference her.

The idea was received with a lot of enthusiasm.

Michelle was irate. *How dare he?* After the meeting, the man approached her and said, "Look, I meant no disrespect, but I wanted to test whether they were rejecting your idea, or you."

The answer was clear. Michelle quit, and walked away from an important initiative that she had conceived and raised.

THE COST OF UNTAPPED GENIUS

Women are the greatest untapped natural resource on the planet.

—REGENA THOMASHAUER

Every day and every year, companies are bleeding unrealized female genius. We will never know where these opportunities could have taken us had those women not been shut down, intimidated, or made to feel uncomfortable.

Most organizations operate in patriarchal ways without realizing it. Just like many men, many women uphold the old game and reinforce the walls of the organization's invisible inner prison—oftentimes with more vigor—because any deviation from the status quo is extremely threatening to the security systems of their own invisible inner prisons. Conversely, there are many people across the gender continuum who are waking up to their own imprisonment and are craving and actively searching for better ways to live and work as whole, authentic human beings. Because the old way takes an enormous toll.

I've had hundreds of conversations with women across various industries who are forthcoming and candid about the cost of PSD perpetrated by their companies. Men are seen as assertive when they speak up; women are seen as aggressive. When a woman asserts her boundary, she's labeled a bitch. In the medical field, women physicians are often mistaken for nurses. In venture capital presentations, women are assumed to be men's assistants. A gender stereotype that nails women on the cross of being "caring" and "nurturing" sustains an expectation that we will carry responsibilities outside of our scope of duties. Women are under greater scrutiny in leadership roles. Many women have to deal with sexual harassment in their workplaces and are often rumored to have slept their way to the top. All of these keep the PSD machine going, that is extremely taxing on women and ends up costing organizations big—in lost and underutilized talent, high turnover, poor public image, lawsuits, and higher medical and legal costs.

Women are twice as likely as men to be diagnosed with mental illness. A 2017 Mental Health America study of 17,000 employees across nineteen industries tied poor mental health to people's experiences in the US workplaces.[30] According to the World Health Organization, depression and anxiety cost the global economy over US $1 trillion per year in lost productivity.[31] Without awareness of what creates these problems, how workplace factors may be contributing to them, and how to prevent and skillfully address them, businesses inadvertently perpetuate the issues.

Simply employing and promoting women does not mean that a company has set the conditions to unlock and nurture their genius and well-being.

Research from the Boston Consulting Group shows that women-led teams have a 35 percent higher return on investment than all-male teams.[32] Imagine what women would be able to accomplish if we removed the daily stressors of PSD. Women swim upstream against unconscious biases that play out in every conversation and interaction. If we removed these invisible walls, how much more would women be able to tap into their authentic genius? How much greater would the company's return on investment be—not just in revenue, but in creativity, vision, industry disruption, innovation, customer satisfaction and loyalty, employee retention, health, happiness, and fulfillment?

---

30 "Mind the Workplace," *Mental Health America Survey,* 2017.

31 "Mental Health in the Workplace," *World Health Organization,* 2019.

32 Katie Abouzahr, "Why Women-Owned Startups Are a Better Bet," *BCG,* June 6, 2018.

FOLLOWING THE CYCLES

Part of setting the conditions for women to perform optimally is recognizing that patriarchal structures were not built with women in mind. As a result, our needs don't fit in. Women's genius requires a different pace and structure than the patriarchal culture dictates.

Women's creativity is not linear. Women—and all humans—have naturally occurring cycles and require variable conditions to perform optimally. Some people work better in solitude while others thrive in teams. Some people flourish in office environments while others produce much better while working remotely. There are natural cycles of productivity throughout the day that may not always fit within a nine-to-five structure.

The invitation is to see the box we're operating within, and to recognize its limitations. When each individual can recognize how to ride rather than override her own waves of naturally occurring productivity and creativity, she can allow the space to fully express herself and shine. The more we recognize and honor the conditions in which people's genius can be optimally expressed, the better outcomes we create for our teams.

Organizations, just like individuals, often operate in survival rather than thriving mode. The company culture then further reinforces the survival wiring within each individual employee. When we begin shifting culture, we create change both internally and externally.

When we shift the question from *how much can we*

bear? to *how good can it get?* we open up space to shift the company's policies, visions, direction and execution to a state of thriving.

The game of *how good can it get?* can become the new organizing principle of your company, and it can put your organization in a position to lead in the new economy. People are no longer settling for transactional relationships with companies. They want to do business with organizations that stand for something. People are seeking out companies that are on the same journey they are. As employees and consumers tap into the full potential of their own lives, talents, and genius, your company can be right there with them, providing the best work environment, customer experience, and outcomes, with the best products and services. That kind of external change is not possible without internal shifts.

CONCLUSION

And then the day came when the risk to remain tight in the
bud was more painful than the risk it took to blossom.

—ANAÏS NIN

THE POET AND MYSTIC RUMI HAS A POEM IN WHICH
he contemplates a conversation with an embryo. He
tells the embryo about the amazing, juicy, exciting,
mind-blowing wonders of the world. He describes the
tastes, smells, colors, joys, and pleasures of places, people,
and celebrations. He speaks of delightful foods and starry
skies. And then Rumi asks the embryo, why does she
choose to stay in the dark instead of coming out into this
big, beautiful world?

To which the embryo responds, "There is no 'other
world.' I only know what I've experienced. You must be
hallucinating."

As I look back at my life a year ago and look ahead to

what wants to burst forth in my life in the next year, I am amazed and humbled at how different my reality is now, from what I thought was possible a few months back. I know that the reality I am bringing forth in the next few months will blow the mind of the present-time me.

I am filled with compassion for the person I was. She was scared. She was on the precipice of big leaps: closing her successful psychology practice in New York, moving her daughter and herself to Arizona, and starting a business that didn't have a proven concept. Nothing was a proven concept for her. She was taking a leap of faith fueled by desire. She had no blueprints to lead the way ahead; only the pain of the invisible prison she was leaving behind.

She had no guarantees that the leap would be successful.

I have so much respect for my past self for being able to follow the pull of that desire. I had felt the walls of the invisible prison closing down on me. I couldn't breathe, I couldn't smile, and I couldn't feel fully alive. I'm so grateful for the search, the journey that awakened my desire for happiness and fulfillment and activated the DNA of freedom.

I'm grateful that the pull of the excitement of the new game became greater than the pull of the safety of the old.

Now, as I enjoy the love, the health, the business I was able to grow, I know that I am just getting started. My jailbreak work continues every day. If there's anything I have learned on this journey, it's that to go higher, we need to dig deeper.

With each new inhale of expansion and desire that I breathe into my life, there is a fuller exhale that taps into yet another layer of confinement. I'm grateful that I now have the awareness, the capacity, and the strategies to keep healing my way to freedom.

As each layer is revealed and liberated, new dimensions of my life open up. Whole new levels of joy, happiness, and vitality, and a fuller range of emotional expression become available. There are exponential wins to celebrate every step of the way.

My blossoming took me here, to a December afternoon in Tucson, Arizona. I just finished a call with a client, and I'm getting ready to release a new episode of my podcast—another amazing interview with another remarkable woman leader talking about Patriarchy Stress Disorder. I sat underneath a beautiful tree in my backyard, and I relished in the feeling of the sunlight on my skin. I felt the soft wind. I smelled desert flowers in the air. A feeling of contentment, of very deep well-being, overcame me.

It was like champagne bubbles of joy moving through me. I felt an expansion and warmth in my chest, relaxation in my arms and shoulders and my face. My eyes were smiling. I just wanted to stand up and dance—and so I did. I was filled with gratitude, and at the same time, with disbelief that this level of fulfillment and happiness was possible for anyone, let alone possible for me.

As someone who had two major depressive episodes and suffered from incapacitating anxiety for years, I had no reference point for this level of full-bodied joy. I had no role models for contentment. Like the embryo in Rumi's poem, I never believed for a moment that this existed in the world, or that I would ever live to experience it.

I followed the breadcrumbs of my joy—that I stole from the grips of inherited and well-practiced suffering—every step of the way.

And on this December afternoon, I see that these crumbs have become a delicious feast of my consciously created life. I'm now able to enjoy it as much as I desire, and I have the capacity to do it.

This is my new normal.

It can be yours, too.

ABOUT THE AUTHOR

DR. VALERIE REIN is a psychologist, women's mental health expert, and business consultant, helping people achieve the best ROI by achieving the best mental health—without therapy. Dr. Valerie specializes in uncovering the hidden traumas that hold hostage people's best work, relationships, and well-being, and effectively heal them with a powerful mind-body methodology. She holds an EdM in Psychological Counseling from Columbia University and a PhD from the Institute of Transpersonal Psychology. Dr. Valerie is a sought-after speaker at conferences and companies committed to diversity and inclusion, leadership development, and unlocking people's potential.

DISCLAIMER

THE INFORMATION PROVIDED IN THIS BOOK IS FOR educational purposes only and is not intended to diagnose, treat, cure, or prevent any disease or condition. It is not intended to be a substitute for professional advice, diagnosis, or treatment provided by your own medical or mental healthcare provider. Although the author is a psychologist, reading this book does not create a provider-client or therapist-patient relationship with her.

While best efforts have been used in preparing this book, the author and publisher make no representations or warranties of any kind and assume no liabilities of any kind with respect to the accuracy or completeness of the contents and specifically disclaim any implied warranties of merchantability or fitness of use for a particular purpose. References are provided for informational purposes only and do not constitute endorsement of any websites or other sources. Some names and identifying details have been changed to protect the privacy of individuals.

Neither the author nor the publisher shall be held liable or responsible to any person or entity with respect to any loss or incidental or consequential damages caused, or alleged to have been caused, directly or indirectly, by the information or programs contained herein. No warranty may be created or extended by sales representatives or written sales materials. Every person and company is different and the advice and strategies contained herein may not be suitable for your situation. You should seek the services of a competent professional before beginning any improvement program.

Printed in Great Britain
by Amazon

57932177R00166